PROGRAMMING LANGUAGES SERIES 4

2 BOOKS IN 1" A BEGINNERS GUIDE TO LEARN HTML PROGRAMMING STEP-BY-STEP"

By John Davis

1

HTML1

HTML2

MICROSOFT ACCESS

HTML PROGRAMMING

A BEGINNERS GUIDE TO HTML PROGRAMMING LANGUAGE, WEB DESIGN AND MORE....

by John Davis

Other than basic content, HTML and XHTML give you an approach to show exceptional content characters that you may not ordinarily have the option to remember for your source record or that have different purposes. A genuine model is the not exactly or opening section image. In HTML, it ordinarily means the beginning of a tag, so on the off chance that you embed it basically as a component of your content, the program will get confounded and presumably misconstrue your archive.

For both HTML and XHTML, the ampersand character teaches the program to utilize an uncommon character, officially known as a character substance. For instance, the order embeds that bothersome not as much as image into the delivered text. Additionally, it embeds the more noteworthy than image, and & embeds an ampersand. There can be no spaces between the ampersand, the element name, and the required, following semicolon. (Semicolons aren't unique characters; you don't have to utilize an ampersand grouping to show a semicolon ordinarily.)

CHAPTER 1

Comments

Remarks are another sort of printed content that show up in the source HTML report, yet are not delivered by the client's program. Remarks fall between the exceptional markups components. Programs overlook the content between the remark character arrangements.

There should be a space after the underlying and going before the last, however else you can put almost anything inside the remark. The greatest exemption for this standard is that the HTML standard doesn't allow you to settle remarks.

Web Explorer additionally allows you to put remarks inside an exceptional comment tag. Everything between the comment and comment tag is overlooked by Internet Explorer, however any remaining programs will show the remark to the client. In view of this unfortunate conduct, we don't suggest utilizing the comment tag for remarks. All things being equal, consistently utilize the arrangements to delimit remarks.

Other than the conspicuous utilization of remarks for source documentation, many web workers use remarks to exploit highlights explicit to the archive worker programming. These workers examine the record for explicit character successions inside traditional HTML remarks and afterward play out some activity dependent on the orders installed in the remarks. The activity may be pretty much as basic as including text from another record (known as a worker side incorporate) or as mind boggling as executing different orders on the worker to create the archive substance powerfully.

Each HTML report ought to adjust to the HTML SGML DTD, the conventional Document Type Definition that characterizes the HTML standard. The DTD characterizes the labels and grammar that are utilized to make a HTML archive. You can advise the program which DTD your archive consents to by putting an extraordinary SGML (Standard Summed up Markup Language) order in the primary line of the report.

This mysterious message shows that your record is expected to be agreeable with the HTML 4.01 last DTD characterized by the World Wide Web Consortium (W3C). Different variants of the DTD characterize more limited renditions of the HTML standard, and not all programs support all adaptations of the HTML DTD. Indeed, determining some other doctype may make the program confuse your archive while showing it for the client. It's likewise muddled what doctype to utilize while remembering for the HTML record the different labels that are not guidelines, but rather are mainstream highlights of a famous program - the Netscape augmentations, for example, or even the expostulated HTML 3.0 norm, for which a DTD was rarely delivered.

Basically nobody goes before their HTML reports with the SGML doctype order. In view of the disarray of forms and norms, we don't suggest that you incorporate the prefix with your HTML archives all things considered.

Then again, we do unequivocally suggest that you incorporate the legitimate doctype proclamation in your XHTML archives, in conformance with XML principles. Peruse next sections to become familiar with DTDs and the new Extensible Markup Language guidelines.

The Tag

As we saw before, the html labels serve to delimit the start and finishing of a record. Since the normal program can without much of a stretch induce from the encased source that it is a HTML archive, you don't actually have to remember the tag for your source HTML record.

All things considered, it's viewed as great structure to incorporate this tag so different devices, especially more unremarkable content preparing ones, can perceive your record as a HTML report. At any rate, the presence of the start and finishing html labels guarantees that the start or the finish of the archive haven't been accidentally erased. Also, XHTML requires the html tag.

Inside the html tag and its end tag are the archive's head and body. Inside the head, you'll discover labels that distinguish the archive and characterize its place inside a report assortment. Inside the body is the genuine archive content, characterized by labels that decide the design and presence of the report text. As you would expect, the archive head is contained inside a head tag and the body is inside a body tag, the two of which are characterized later.

The body tag might be supplanted by a frameset tag, characterizing at least one showcase outlines that, thus, contain genuine report content. By a long shot, the most widely recognized type of the html tag in HTML records is essentially.

At the point when the html tag shows up without the rendition property, the HTML archive worker and program expect the adaptation of HTML utilized in this record is provided to the program by the worker.

The dir attribute

The dir quality indicates in which course the program should deliver text inside the containing component. At the point when utilized inside the html tag, it decides how text will be introduced inside the whole archive. At the point when utilized inside another tag, it controls the content's heading for simply the substance of that tag.

Naturally, the estimation of this tag is ltr, demonstrating that text is introduced to the client left-to-right. Utilize the other worth, rtl, to show text option to-left for dialects like Chinese or Hebrew. Of course, the outcomes rely upon your substance and the program's help of HTML 4.Netscape and Internet Explorer Versions 4 and prior overlook the dir property. The HTML 4-agreeable Internet Explorer Version 5 essentially right-legitimizes dir=rtl text, despite the fact that on the off chance that you'll see the program moves the accentuation (the time frame) to the opposite side of the sentence:

The lang attribute

At the point when included inside the html tag, the lang trait indicates the language you've commonly utilized inside the record. At the point when utilized inside different labels, the lang trait indicates the language you utilized inside that label's substance. Preferably, the program will utilize lang to all the more likely render the content for the client.

Set the estimation of the lang quality to an ISO-639 standard two-character language code. You may likewise demonstrate a vernacular by following the ISO language code with a scramble and a subcode name. For instance, "en" is the ISO language code for English; "en-US" is the finished code for US English. Other regular language codes incorporate "fr" (French), "de" (German), "it" (Italian), "nl" (Dutch), "el" (Greek), "es" (Spanish), "pt" (Portuguese), "ar" (Arabic), "he" (Hebrew), "ru" (Russian), "zh" (Chinese), "ja" (Japanese), and "hey" (Hindi).

The version attribute

The variant quality characterizes the HTML standard rendition used to create the archive. Its worth, for HTML Version 4.01, should peruse precisely:

As a rule, variant data inside the html tag is more difficulty than it is worth, and this trait has been censured in HTML 4. Genuine creators ought to rather utilize a SGML doctype tag toward the start of their records, this way:

The Document Header

The record header depicts the different properties of the report, including its title, position inside the Web, and relationship with different archives. A large portion of the information contained inside the report header is never really delivered as substance obvious to the client.

The head Tag

The head label serves to epitomize the other header labels. Spot it toward the start of your record, soon after the html tag and before the body or frameset tag. Both the head tag and its comparing finishing head can be unambiguously induced by the program thus can be securely overlooked from an archive. In any case, we do urge you to remember them for your archives, since they advance meaningfulness and backing report mechanization.

The dir and lang attributes

The dir and lang ascribes help stretch out HTML and XHTML to a worldwide crowd.

The profile attribute

Frequently, the header of a record contains various Meta labels used to pass on extra data about the report to the program. Later on, creators may utilize predefined profiles of standard record metadata to all the more likely depict their reports. The profile characteristic supplies the URL of the profile related with the current archive.

The arrangement of a profile and how it very well may be utilized by a program are not yet characterized; this trait is basically a placeholder for future turn of events.

Programs don't extraordinarily arrange title message and overlook something besides text inside the title start and end labels. For example, they will disregard any pictures or connections to different reports.

Here's a considerably barer barebones illustration of a substantial HTML archive to feature the header and title labels; watch what happens when Netscape shows it.

What's in a title?

Choosing the correct title is pivotal to characterizing an archive and guaranteeing that it very well may be successfully utilized inside the World Wide Web.

Remember that clients can get to every one of your reports in an assortment in almost any request and autonomously of each other. Each archive's title ought to in this manner characterize the report both inside the setting of your different records just as on its own benefits.

Titles that incorporate references to record sequencing are typically unseemly. Straightforward titles, similar to "Section 2" or "Part VI" do little to assist a client with understanding what the archive may contain. More unmistakable titles, like Advanced Square Dancing" or Churchill's Youth and Adulthood," pass on both a feeling of spot inside a bigger arrangement of archives and explicit substance that welcomes the user to peruse on.

Self-referential titles likewise aren't extremely helpful. A title like "My Home Page" is totally without content, as are titles like "Input Page" or "Mainstream Links." You need a title to pass on a feeling of substance and reason so clients can choose, in light of the title alone, if to visit that page. "The Kumquat Lover's Home Page" is spellbinding and prone to attract admirers of the harsh organic product, as are "Kumquat Lover's Feedback Page" and "Well known Links Frequented by Kumquat Lovers."

Individuals invest a lot of energy making records for the Web, regularly just to waste that exertion with an uninviting, insufficient title. As extraordinary programming that naturally gathers joins for clients turns out to be more common on the Web, the solitary graphic expression related with your pages when they are embedded into some huge connection data set will be the title you decide for them. We must accentuate this as much as possible: take care to choose expressive, helpful, setting free titles for every one of your records.

Related Header Tags

Different labels you may incorporate inside the head label manage explicit parts of report creation, the board, connecting, computerization, or design. That is the reason we just notice them here and portray them in more prominent detail in other, more fitting areas and sections of this book.

The Document Body

The record body is the meat of the matter; it's the place where you put the substance of your report. The body tag delimits the archive body.

The body Tag

Inside HTML 4 and XHTML, the body tag has various ascribes that control the tone and foundation of your report. Different programs, have stretched out the tag to give considerably more noteworthy power over your record's appearance.

Anything inside the body tag and its consummation partner body is called body content. The least difficult archive may have just an arrangement of text sections inside the body tag. More perplexing reports will incorporate vigorously organized content, graphical figures, tables, and an assortment of enhancements.

Since the situation of the body and body labels can be gathered by the program, they can securely be excluded from the report. Nonetheless, similar to the html and head labels, we suggest that you incorporate the body labels in your archive to make them all the more effectively meaningful and viable.

The different ascribes for the body tag can be approximately gathered into three sets: those that give you some authority over the report's appearance, those that partner programmable capacities with the actual archive, and those that mark and distinguish the body for later reference. We address the appearance ascribes (alink, foundation, bgcolor, bgproperties, leftmargin, connect, text, topmargin, and vlink); the class and style credits for falling templates; JavaScript templates and the automatic credits (the "on-occasion" ones) the language credits (dir and lang) prior and the ID ascribes (id and title).

Frames

The HTML and XHTML norms characterize an exceptional sort of report wherein you supplant the body tag with at least one frameset labels. This purported outline record isolates the showcase window into at least one autonomous windows, each showing an alternate archive. We completely portray this development.

Editorial Markup

HTML 4.0 presented two new labels that can help gatherings of creators team up in the improvement of archives and keep up some similarity to publication and variant control. The supplement (ins) and erase (del) labels let you assign segments of your record's body as either new or added content, or assign old stuff that ought to be supplanted. Also, with exceptional credits, you may show when you rolled out the improvement (date time) and a reference to a report that may clarify the change (refer to).

The ins and del Tags

The ins and del labels let creators set off bits of body substance they expect to add to or erase from the current form of their report. HTML 4/XHTML-consistent programs show the substance of the ins or del labels in some extraordinary manner so users can rapidly filter the report for the changes.

Netscape 4 and prior variants disregard the labels, as did Internet Explorer 4 and prior forms. The most current variants of Internet Explorer (Version 5) and Netscape (Version 6) utilize regular publication markings by underlining embedded content and striking out erased text.

The cite attribute

That refer to ascribe allows you to report the purposes behind the addition or cancellation. Its worth should be a URL that focuses to some other archive that clarifies the embedded content. How refer to gets treated by a program is an inquiry for what's to come.

The date time attribute

Albeit the justification the change is significant, knowing when a change was made is regularly more significant. The date time trait for the ins and del labels takes a solitary worth: an exceptionally encoded date and time stamp.

The thorough arrangement for the date time esteem is YYYY-MM-DDThh:mm:ssTZD. The parts are:

• YYYY is the year, like 2020 or 2021.

• MM is the month; 02 for February through 12 for December.

• DD is the day; 01 through 31.

• T is a necessary character assigning the start of the time section of the stamp.

• hh is the hour in 24-hour design; 00 (12 PM) through 23 (11 P.M.). (Add an after colon in the event that you incorporate the minutes.)

• mm are the minutes at the top of the hour; 00 through 59. (Add an after colon on the off chance that you incorporate the seconds.)

• ss are the seconds; 00 through 59.

• TZD is the time region designator. It tends to be one of three qualities: Z, demonstrating Greenwich Mean Time, or the hours, minutes, and seconds prior (-) or after (+) Coordinated Universal Time (UTC) where time is comparative with the time in Greenwich, England.

The class, dir, event, id, lang, style, title, and events attributes

There are a few almost general ascribes for the numerous HTML and XHTML labels. These ascribes give you a typical method to distinguish (title) and mark (id) a label's substance for later reference or mechanized treatment; to change the substance's showcase qualities (class, style); and to reference the language utilized (lang) and related course the content should stream (dir). There are additionally input occasions that may occur in and around the labeled substance that you may respond to through an on-occasion characteristic and some programming.

Using Editorial Markup

The employments of ins and del are clear to any individual who has utilized a "standard" report or structure, or who has teamed up with others in the arrangement of a record.

For instance, law offices normally have an assortment of online authoritative records that are exceptionally finished for every customer. Law assistants normally do the "fill in," and the last record gets evaluated by a legal counselor. To feature where the agent made changes in the record so they are promptly obvious to the analyst, utilize the ins tag to demonstrate the assistant's additional content and the del tag to stamp the content that was supplanted. Alternatively utilize refer to and date time qualities to demonstrate when and why the progressions were made.

The publication markup labels could likewise be utilized by altering instruments to indicate how records were adjusted as creators make changes throughout some undefined time frame. With the right utilization of refer to and date time ascribes, it is feasible to reproduce an adaptation of an archive from a particular point on schedule.

The bdo Tag

As we've referenced before, the creators of the HTML 4 standard have put forth a deliberate attempt to incorporate standard ways web specialists (programs) should treat and show the various human dialects and tongues. Likewise, the HTML 4 norm and its descendants XHTML contain the all-inclusive dir and lang ascribes that let you unequivocally exhort the program that the entire record or explicit labeled sections inside it are in a specific language. These language-related ascribes, at that point, may influence some show qualities; for instance, the dir property advises the program to compose the words across the showcase from one or the other left to right (dir=ltr), with respect to most Western dialects, or option to left (dir=rtl), concerning numerous Asian dialects.

The different Unicode and ISO guidelines for language encoding and show may strife with your best expectations. Specifically, the substance of some different records, for example, a MIME-encoded document, as of now might be appropriately arranged and your report may misadvise the program to fix that encoding. Henceforth, the HTML 4 and XHTML principles have the bdo tag. With it, you supersede any current and acquired dir details. Furthermore, with the label's required dir trait, you authoritatively determine the bearing where the label's substance ought to be shown.

In fact, the impacts of the bdo tag are somewhat exclusive and the chances to utilize it as of now are uncommon, especially thinking about that the second most famous program doesn't yet uphold it.

Text Basics

Any fruitful introduction, even a smart book, ought to have its content coordinated into an alluring, compelling archive. Coordinating content into appealing reports is HTML and XHTML's strength. The dialects give you various apparatuses that help you shape your content and make yourself clear. They additionally help structure your record with the goal that your intended interest group has simple admittance to your words.

Continuously remember while planning your archives (same story, different day!) that the markup labels, especially as to message, just prompt - they don't direct - how a program will eventually deliver the report. Delivering changes from one program to another. Try not to get excessively caught with attempting to get the perfect look and format. Your endeavors may and most likely will be ruined by the program.

Divisions and Paragraphs

Like most content processors, a program wraps the words it finds to fit the flat width of its review window. Broaden the program's window and words naturally stream up to fill the more extensive lines. Crush the window and words wrap downwards.

In contrast to most content processors, notwithstanding, HTML and XHTML utilize unequivocal division (div), passage (p), and line-break (br) labels to control the arrangement and stream of text. Return characters, albeit very helpful for intelligibility of the source archive, regularly are disregarded by the program - creators should utilize the br tag to unequivocally power a typical book line break. The p tag, while likewise playing out the assignment, conveys with it importance and impacts past a basic line break.

The div tag is somewhat unique. Initially systematized in the HTML 3.2 norm, div was remembered for the language to be a straightforward authoritative apparatus - to isolate the report into discrete segments - who's to some degree heartless significance implied not many creators utilized it. In any case, ongoing developments - arrangement, styles, and the id trait for archive referring to and mechanization - presently let you all the more unmistakably mark and accordingly characterize singular segments of your records, just as control the arrangement and presence of those segments. These highlights inhale genuine life and significance into the div tag.

By partner an id and a class name with the different areas of your record, each delimited by a tag and qualities (you can do likewise with different labels like p, as well), you not just mark those divisions for later reference by a hyperlink and for robotized handling and the board (gather all the book index divisions, for example), yet you may likewise characterize extraordinary, unmistakable presentation styles for those segments of your report. For example, you may characterize one divisional class for your archive's theoretical, another for the body, a third for the decision, and a fourth divisional class for the list of sources.

Each class, at that point, may be given an alternate presentation definition in a record level or remotely related template: the theoretical indented and in an italic typeface, (for example, div.abstract {left-edge: +0.5in; text style: italic}); the body in a left-defended roman typeface; the end like the theoretical; and the book index consequently numbered and arranged properly.

We give an itemized portrayal of templates, classes, and their applications.

The div Tag

As characterized in the HTML 4.01 and XHTML 1.0 principles, the div label partitions your record into discrete, unmistakable segments. It could be utilized carefully as a hierarchical apparatus, with such a designing related with it; it turns out to be more successful on the off chance that you add the id and class ascribes to mark the division. The div tag may likewise be joined with the adjust trait to control the arrangement of entire areas of your report's substance in the presentation and with the numerous automatic "on" ascribes for client collaboration.

The align attribute in the div tag

The adjust quality for div positions the encased substance to either the left (default), focus, or right of the showcase. Furthermore, you can indicate legitimize to adjust both the left and right edges of the content. The div tag might be settled, and the arrangement of the settled div label outweighs the containing div tag. Further, other settled arrangement labels, for example, center, adjusted sections, or exceptionally adjusted table columns and cells, abrogate the impact of div. Like the adjust property for different labels, it is belittled in the HTML and XHTML norms in reverence to template based format controls.

The nowrap attribute

Upheld simply by Internet Explorer, the nowrap quality stifles programmed word wrapping of the content inside the division. Line breaks will just happen where you have put carriage returns in your source report.

While the nowrap quality presumably doesn't bode well for huge segments of text that would somehow be streamed together on the page, it can make things somewhat simpler when making squares of text with numerous unequivocal line breaks: verse, for instance, or addresses. You don't need to embed every one of those express br labels in a content stream inside

The dir, lang and nowrap attributes

A div nowrap tag. Then again, any remaining programs disregard the nowrap characteristic and happily stream your content together in any case. In the event that you are focusing on just Internet Explorer with your archives, consider utilizing nowrap where required, however else, we can't suggest this trait for general use.

The id attribute

The dir trait allows you to prompt the program concerning which bearing the content should be shown, and the lang characteristic allows you to indicate the language utilized inside the division. Utilize the id property to name the record division extraordinarily for later reference by a hyperlink, template, applet, or other robotized measure. A satisfactory id esteem is any statement encased string that interestingly distinguishes the division and that later can be utilized to reference that archive segment unambiguously. Despite the fact that we're presenting it inside the setting of the div tag, this property can be utilized with practically any tag.

At the point when utilized as a component name, the estimation of the id trait can be added to a URL to address the marked component exceptionally inside the archive. You can mark both enormous parts of substance (through a label like div) and little scraps of text (utilizing a label like i or span). For instance, you may mark the theoretical of a specialized report utilizing div id="abstract". A URL could bounce right to that theoretical by referring to report. At the point when utilized as such, the estimation of the id trait should be special as for any remaining id ascribes inside the report, and every one of the names characterized by any a labels with the name property.

At the point when utilized as a template selector, the estimation of the id quality is the name of a style decide that can be related with the current tag. This gives a second arrangement of determinable style rules, like the different style classes you can make. A tag can utilize both the class and id credits to apply two unique guidelines to a solitary tag. In this use, the name related with the id property should be one of a kind regarding any remaining style IDs inside the current record. A more complete portrayal of style classes and IDs can be found in later sections.

The title attribute

Utilize the discretionary title characteristic and statement encased string worth to connect an engaging expression with the division. Like the id property, the title trait can be utilized with practically any tag and acts also for all labels.

There is no characterized use for the estimation of the title quality, and numerous programs just overlook it. Web Explorer, notwithstanding, will show the title related with any component when the mouse stops over that component. Clever. Utilized effectively, the title property could be utilized as such to give spot help to the different components inside your record.

The class and style attributes

Utilize the style characteristic with the div tag to make an inline style for the substance encased by tag. The class quality allows you to apply the style of a predefined class of the div tag to the substance of this division. The estimation of the class trait is the name of a style characterized in some archive level or remotely characterized template. Furthermore, class-recognized divisions additionally loan themselves well for PC handling of your reports, for example, extraction of all divisions whose class name is "biblio," for instance, for the mechanized gathering of an expert catalog.

Event attributes in HTML

The numerous client related occasions that may occur in and around a division, for example, when a client snaps or double taps the mouse inside its showcase space, are perceived by the program in the event that it adjusts to the current HTML or XHTML principles. With the separate "on" characteristic and worth, you may respond to that occasion by showing a client exchange box, or enacting some media occasion.

The p label flags the beginning of a section. That is not notable even by some veteran website admins, on the grounds that it runs outlandish to what exactly we've generally expected for a fact. Most word processors we're comfortable with utilize only one extraordinary character, regularly the return character, to flag the finish of a passage. In HTML and XHTML, each section should begin with p and closes with the comparing p tag. And keeping in mind that a succession of newline characters in a content processor-showed report makes a vacant passage for everyone, programs commonly disregard everything except the main section tag.

By and by, with HTML you can overlook the beginning p tag toward the start of the primary passage, and the p tag toward the finish of sections: they can be suggested from different labels that happen in the report, and henceforth securely excluded.

Notice that we have excluded the passage start tag (p) for the primary section or any end section labels whatsoever in the HTML model; they can be unambiguously derived by the program and are in this manner superfluous.

By and large, you'll see that human record creators will in general discard proposed labels at whatever point conceivable while programmed report generators will in general embed them. That might be on the grounds that the product originators would not like to risk having their item rebuked by contenders as not holding fast to the HTML standard, despite the fact that we're parting apparent aim of-the-law hairs here. Feel free to be insubordinate: preclude that first passage's p tag and don't really think about section finishing p labels, given, obviously, that your report's design and clearness are not traded off. That is, the length of you know that XHTML grimaces seriously on such laxity.

CHAPTER 2

Paragraph rendering

While experiencing another section (p) tag, a program ordinarily embeds one clear line in addition to some additional vertical space into the archive prior to beginning the new passage. The program at that point gathers every one of the words and, if present, inline pictures into the new section, overlooking driving and following spaces (not spaces between words, obviously) and return characters in the source text. The program programming at that point streams the subsequent grouping of words and pictures into a section that fits inside the edges of its presentation window, naturally creating line breaks on a case by case basis to wrap the content inside the window. For instance, look at how a program orchestrates the content into lines and sections to how the first model is imprinted on the page. The program may likewise consequently hyphenate long words, and the section might be full-defended to extend the line of words out towards the two edges.

The net outcome is that you don't need to stress over line length, word wrap, and line breaks when forming your reports. The program will take any discretionary grouping of words and pictures and show a pleasantly organized passage.

On the off chance that you need to control line length and breaks expressly, consider utilizing a preformatted text block with the pre tag. In the event that you need to drive a line break, utilize the br tag.

The align attribute in paragraph rendering

Most programs consequently left-legitimize another section. To change this conduct, HTML 4 and XHTML give you the adjust property for the p tag and give four sorts of substance support: left, right, focus, or legitimize.

Notice in the HTML model that the section arrangement stays basically until the program experiences another p tag or a closure p tag. We purposely left out a last p tag in the guide to delineate the impacts of the p end tag on passage defense. Other body components may likewise upset the current passage arrangement and cause ensuing sections to return to the default left arrangement, including structures, headers, tables, and most other body content-related labels.

Note that the adjust property is expostulated in HTML 4 and XHTML in regard to template based arrangements.

The dir and lang attributes in paragraph rendering

The dir allows you to exhort the program concerning which course the content inside the section should be shown, and the lang quality allows you to indicate the language utilized inside that passage. The dir and lang ascribes are upheld by the mainstream programs, despite the fact that there are no practices characterized for a particular language.

The class, id, style, and title attributes

Utilize the id characteristic to make a mark for the passage that can later be utilized to unambiguously reference that section in a hyperlink focus, for computerized look, as a template selector, and with a large group of different applications.

Utilize the discretionary title property and statement encased string worth to give a clear expression to the passage.

Utilize the style characteristic with the p tag to make an inline style for the section's substance. The class property allows you to name the passage with a name that alludes to a predefined class of the p label proclaimed in some record level or remotely characterized template. Furthermore, class-distinguished sections loan themselves well for PC preparing of your archives, for example, extraction of all passages whose class name is "reference," for instance, for mechanized get together of an expert rundown of references.

The title and event attributes

Like with divisions, there are numerous client started occasions, for example, when a client snaps or double taps inside its presentation space, that are perceived by the program in the event that it adjusts to the current HTML or XHTML principles. With the individual "on" quality and worth, you may respond to that occasion by showing a client discourse box or initiating some media occasion.

Allowed paragraph usage

You may indicate a section just inside a square, alongside different passages, records, structures, and preformatted text. All in all, this implies that sections can show up where a progression of text is fitting, for example, in the body of a report, a component in a rundown, etc. In fact, sections can't show up inside a header, anchor, or other component whose substance is carefully text-as it were. Practically speaking, most programs overlook this limitation and arrangement the passage as a piece of the containing component.

Headings

Clients have a hard enough time perusing what's shown on a screen. A long progression of text, whole by title, captions, and different headers, crosses the eyes and numbs the brain, also the way that it makes it almost difficult to examine the content for a particular point.

You ought to consistently break a progression of text into a few more modest segments inside at least one headings. There are six degrees of headings that you can use to structure a book stream into a more comprehensible, more sensible record. Also, there are an assortment of graphical and text-style deceives that help partition your archive and make its substance more open just as more clearly to clients.

Heading Tags

The encased content inside a heading commonly is exceptionally delivered by the program, contingent on the showcase innovation accessible to it. The program may decide to focus, encourage, grow, stress, underline, or change the shade of headings to make each stand apart inside the archive. What's more, to impede the most monotonous journalists, clients, also, regularly can adjust how a program will deliver the various headings.

At long last, remember to incorporate the proper heading end labels in your archive. The program will not embed one naturally for you, and overlooking the closure tag for a heading can have grievous ramifications for your report.

The align attribute in heading tags

The default heading arrangement for most programs is left. Like the div and p labels, you can change this arrangement with the adjust property and one of the qualities left, focus, right, or legitimize.

Legitimize an incentive for adjust isn't upheld yet by any program, and don't hold your breath. The adjust property is censured in HTML 4 and XHTML in concession to template based controls.

The dir and lang credits

The dir characteristic allows you to prompt the program regarding which course the content inside that section should be shown, and lang allows you to indicate the language utilized inside the heading.

The class, id, style, and title credits

Utilize the id property to make a mark for the heading that can later be to use to unambiguously reference that heading in a hyperlink focus, for robotized look, as a template selector, and with a large group of different applications.

Utilize the discretionary title characteristic and statement encased string worth to give an unmistakable expression to the heading.

Utilize the style trait with the making a beeline for make an inline style for the headings' substance. The class property allows you to name the heading with a name that alludes to a predefined class announced in some report level or remotely characterized template.

Occasion attributes

Every client started occasion that may occur in and around a heading each are perceived by the program on the off chance that it adjusts to the HTML or XHTML guidelines. With the separate "on" property and worth, you may respond to that occasion by showing a client discourse box or actuating some interactive media occasion.

Appropriate Use of Headings

It's acceptable structure to rehash your archive's title in the primary heading tag, since the title you indicate toward the start of your record doesn't show up in the client's principle show window. The title should coordinate with the one in the archive's head. The accompanying HTML section is a genuine illustration of rehashing the record's title in the header and in the body of the archive:

While the program may put the title some place in the archive window and may likewise utilize it to make bookmarks or hotlist sections, all of which enigmatically are some place on the client's work area, the level three title heading in the model will consistently show up at the earliest reference point of the record. It fills in as an obvious title to the record paying little mind to how the program handles the title label substance. Also, not at all like the title text, the heading title will show up toward the start of the main page should the client choose for print the record.

In the model, we decided to utilize a level three heading whose delivered textual style commonly is slightly bigger than the standard archive text. Levels one and two are bigger still and frequently somewhat domineering. You ought to pick a degree of heading that you find helpful and appealing and utilize that level reliably all through your records.

Whenever you have set up the high level heading for your record, utilize extra headings at something very similar or lower level all through to add construction and "scan ability" to the archive. On the off chance that you utilize a level three heading for the record title, break your archive into a few segments utilizing level four headings. On the off chance that you have the desire to partition your content further, think about utilizing a level two heading for the title, level three for the segment dividers, and level four for the subsections.

Using Headings for Smaller Text

Creators regularly utilize the last two sizes for standard text, similar to a disclaimer or a copyright notice. It's gotten very mainstream to utilize the more modest content in Tables of Contents or home pages that show a site's substance. Examination with headings to get the impact you need. Perceive how a normal program delivers the copyright reference in the accompanying example HTML portion.

Allowed Heading Content

Practically speaking, notwithstanding, text style or style changes may not produce results inside a heading, since the actual heading recommends a textual style change inside the program.

There is inescapable maltreatment of the heading labels as a system for changing the text style of a whole record. In fact, sections, records, and other square components are not permitted inside a heading and might be mixed up by the program to show the suggested end of the heading. By and by, most programs apply the style of the going to every single contained passage. We debilitate this training since it isn't just an infringement of HTML and XHTML guidelines however generally terrible to take a gander at. Envision if your neighborhood paper printed all the duplicate in title text type!

Assigning enormous segments of text as heading content invalidates the point of the tag. On the off chance that you truly need to change the whole text style or type size of your report, consider rather characterizing a novel style for the tag of your record. This style will be applied to all the substance inside and will make later adjustment of your report style a lot simpler.

Also, we unequivocally suggest that you cautiously test your pages with more than one program and at a few distinct goals. As normal, your text might be intelligible at 320 x 480 goal, yet vanish on a 600 x 800 showcase.

Allowed Heading Usage

Officially, the HTML and XHTML principles permit headings just inside body content. By and by, most programs perceive headings anyplace, organizing the delivered text to fit inside the current component. Altogether cases, the event of a heading means the finish of any previous section or other content component, so you can't utilize the going to change text dimensions in a similar line. Or maybe, use styles to accomplish those intense presentation impacts.

Adding Images to Headings

It is feasible to embed at least one pictures inside your headings, from little slugs or symbols to full-sized logos. Joining a predictable arrangement of headings with relating symbols across a group of reports isn't just outwardly appealing, however a successful method of supporting clients' scrutiny of your record assortment.

Adding a picture to a heading is simple. For instance, the accompanying content puts an "data" symbol inside the "For More Information" heading.

As a rule, pictures inside headings take a gander toward the start of the heading, lined up with the base or center of the heading text.

Changing Text Appearance

Various labels change the presence of and partner covered up significance with text. All in all, these labels can be gathered into two flavors: content-based styles and actual styles.

Moreover, the W3C standard for Cascading Style Sheets is currently very much upheld by the well-known programs, giving another, more thorough route for creators to control the look and format of their archive text. Netscape has additionally executed templates through JavaScript. We portray the tag-based content styles in this section.

Content-Based Styles

Content-based style labels advise the program that the encased content has a particular significance, setting, or utilization. The program at that point organizes the content in a way reliable with that significance, setting, or utilization.

Since textual style is determined through semantic hints, the program can pick a presentation style that is fitting for the client. Since such styles change by region, utilizing content-based styles guarantees that your archives will have significance to a more extensive scope of per users. This is especially significant when a program is focused at daze or disabled per users whose show alternatives are fundamentally not the same as ordinary content or are amazingly restricted somehow or another.

The current HTML and XHTML principles don't characterize an organization for every one of the substance based styles with the exception of that they should be delivered in a way not quite the same as the standard content in a record. The standard doesn't demand that the substance based styles be delivered uniquely in contrast to each other. Practically speaking, you'll see that a significant number of these labels have genuinely clear associations with regular print, having comparable implications and delivered styles, and are delivered in similar style and textual styles by most programs.

Physical Styles

We utilize "plan" a great deal when we talk about content-based style labels. That is on the grounds that the significance passed on by the tag is a higher priority than the manner in which a program shows the content. Now and again, be that as it may, you may need the content to show up expressly in some unique manner - italic or intense, for instance - maybe for lawful or copyright reasons. In those cases, utilize an actual style for the content.

While the propensity with other content preparing frameworks is to control style and appearance expressly, with HTML or XHTML you ought to dodge unequivocal, actual labels besides on uncommon events. Give the program however much context oriented data as could reasonably be expected. Utilize the substance based styles. Despite the fact that current programs may do simply show their content in italic or strong, future programs and different record age instruments may utilize the substance based styles in quite a few imaginative manners.

Content-Based Style Tags

It takes control to utilize the substance based styles, since it is simpler to just consider how your content should look, not really what it might likewise mean. When you begin utilizing content-based styles, your records will be more predictable and better loan themselves to computerized looking and substance arrangement.

HTML's Expanded Font Handling

We obsessed about remembering this part for a noticeable situation inside this section, or consigning it as far as possible. It has a place here on the grounds that the different labels related with the all-encompassing text style model for HTML were essential for the norm. Also, they stay famous with HTML creators, other than being very much upheld by every one of the mainstream programs. However they have been deplored in the HTML 4 and XHTML 1.0 principles, justifying banishing the entire segment to the furthest limit of the part with every one of the implied warnings.

We speculate the W3C needs creators to utilize templates, not intense labels, for unequivocal control of text style styles, tones, and sizes of the content characters. That is the reason these all-encompassing textual style labels and related ascribes have fallen into disgrace. We put this part here on the grounds that we question that most of HTML writers will quit utilizing, nor that the well-known programs will any time before long forsake support for, labels that are in such far and wide use. Simply know about their tricky situation in the language.

The Extended Font Size Model

Rather than total point esteems, the Extended Font Model of HTML 3.2 as upheld by the well-known programs utilizes a general model for estimating textual styles. Sizes range from 1, the littlest, to 7, the biggest; the default (base text style) text dimension is 3.

It is practically difficult to state dependably the real text dimensions utilized for the different virtual sizes. Most programs let the client change the actual text dimension, and the default sizes differ from one program to another. It could be useful to know, in any case, that each virtual size is progressively 20% bigger or more modest than the default text dimension 3. In this manner, text dimension 4 is 20 percent bigger, text dimension 5 is 40 percent bigger, etc., while text dimension 2 is 20 percent more modest and text dimension 1 is 40 percent more modest than text dimension 3.

Better Line-Breaking Rules

In contrast to certain programs, and shockingly, Netscape Navigator and Internet Explorer don't believe labels to be a line-break opportunity. Think about the shocking results to your report's presentation if, while delivering the model portion beneath, the program puts the comma nearby the "du" or the time frame neighboring "df" on a different line. Netscape and Internet Explorer won't.

Addresses

Addresses are an extremely normal component in text records, so there is an uncommon label that separates addresses from the remainder of an archive's book. While this may appear to be somewhat luxurious - addresses have not many designing eccentricities that would require a unique tag - it is an illustration of substance, not arrangement, which is the plan and motivation behind HTML and XHTML markup.

By characterizing text that comprises a location, the creator allows the program to design that text in an alternate way, just as cycle that text in manners accommodating to clients. It additionally makes the substance promptly open to computerize per users and extractors. For example, an online catalog may incorporate tends to the program gathers into a separate report or table, or computerized apparatuses may remove addresses from an assortment of archives to fabricate a different data set of addresses.

Special Character Encoding

Generally, characters inside archives that are not piece of a tag are delivered as is by the program. Nonetheless, a few characters have extraordinary importance and are not straightforwardly delivered, while different characters can't be composed into the source archive from an ordinary console. Uncommon characters need either an exceptional name or a numeric character encoding for consideration in an archive.

Special Characters

As has gotten clear in the conversation and models paving the way to this segment, three characters in source reports have uncommon importance: the not exactly sign, the more prominent than this sign and the ampersand (and). These characters delimit labels and exceptional character references. They'll confound a program whenever left hanging alone or with ill-advised label grammar. So you must make a special effort to incorporate their genuine, exacting characters in your records.

Likewise, you must utilize an uncommon encoding to incorporate twofold quote characters inside a cited string, or when you need to incorporate an extraordinary character that doesn't show up on your console yet is essential for the ISO Latin-1 character set executed and upheld by most programs.

Inserting Special Characters

To remember an uncommon character for your archive, encase either its standard substance name or a pound sign (#) and its numeric situation in the Latin-1 standard character set inside a main ampersand and a completion semicolon, with no spaces in the middle.

The mainstream ASCII character set is a subset of the more exhaustive Latin-1 character set. Formed by the all-around regarded International Organization for Standardization (ISO), the Latin-1 set is a rundown, everything being equal, numbers, accentuation marks, etc., ordinarily utilized by Western language authors, coordinated by number and encoded with unique names? Index F contains the total Latin-1 character set and encoding.

Golly. That is a long clarification for what is actually something basic to do, as the accompanying model shows. The model tells the best way to incorporate a more prominent than sign in a bit of code by utilizing the character's element name. It likewise exhibits how to incorporate a more prominent than sign in your content by referring to its Latin-1 numeric worth.

Rules, Images, and Multimedia

While the collection of most reports is text, a proper flavoring of even standards, pictures, and other interactive media components make for a considerably more welcoming and alluring record. These highlights are not just unnecessary gewgaws that make your records look pretty, as you may already know. Sight and sound components bring HTML and XHTML records alive, giving an element of significant data frequently inaccessible in other media, like print. In this part, we depict in detail how you can embed extraordinary sight and sound components into your records, when their utilization is suitable, and how to try not to try too hard.

You additionally should bounce ahead and skim. There we portray some catch-all labels, the HTML 4 and XHTML standard, which let you embed a wide range of substance and information record types, including media, into your archives.

Horizontal Rules

Level principles give you an approach to isolate segments of your record outwardly. That way, you give per users a perfect, steady, visual sign that one bit of your report has finished and another segment is starting. Level guidelines viably set off little areas of text, delimit report headers and footers, and give extra visual punch to headings inside your archive.

The size attribute

Regularly, programs render flat principles a few pixels thick with an etched, 3D appearance, making the standard look chiseled into the page.

A pixel is one of the numerous minuscule spots that make up the showcase on your PC. While show sizes shift, a decent dependable guideline is that one pixel approaches one point on a 75 speck for every inch show screen. A point is a unit of measure utilized in printing and is generally equivalent to 1/72 of an inch (there are 72.27 focuses in an inch, to be careful). Ordinary typefaces utilized by different programs are typically 12 focuses tall, yielding six lines of text for every inch.

The noshade attribute

You may not need a 3D standard line, leaning toward a level, 2D guideline. Simply add the noshade quality to the tag to take out the impact. No worth is needed with HTML. Use noshade="noshade" with XHTML. Note the distinction in appearance of a "ordinary" 3D principle versus the noshade 2D one in Figure 5-3. (We've additionally overstated the standard's thickness for clear impact, as obvious in the source HTML piece.)

The width attribute

The default rule is drawn across the full width of the view window. You can abbreviate or protract rules with the width quality, making decide lines that are either a flat out number of pixels wide or reach out across a specific level of the current content stream. Most programs naturally focus fractional width rules; see the adjust property to left-or right-legitimize level guidelines.

Notice that the family member (rate) an incentive for the width trait is encased in quotes; the outright (whole number) pixel esteem isn't. Truth be told, the quotes aren't totally important with standard HTML, however since the percent image ordinarily implies that an encoded character follows, inability to encase the percent width esteem in quotes may befuddle different programs and waste a segment of your record. With XHTML, twofold statements are needed around all characteristic qualities.

As a rule, is anything but a smart thought to determine the width of a standard as a definite number of pixels. Program windows change significantly in their width, and what may be a little guideline on one program may be annoyingly enormous on another. Therefore, we suggest indicating rule width as a level of the window width. That way, when the width of the program window changes, the principles hold their equivalent relative size.

51

The width quality is belittled in HTML 4 and XHTML, since its belongings can be accomplished with fitting utilization of templates.

Using Rules to Divide Your Document

Level guidelines give a helpful visual route gadget for you as per users. To utilize heading successfully as a part divider, first decide the number of levels of headings your archive has and how long you anticipate that each section of the document should be. At that point choose which of your headings warrant being separate by a standard.

A level standard can likewise delimit the front matter of an archive, isolating the chapter by chapter guide from the report body, for instance. Utilize a level principle additionally to isolate the report body from a following record, list of sources, or rundown of figures.

Experienced creators additionally utilize level principles to check the start and end of a structure. This is particularly convenient for long structures that make clients look all over the page to see every one of the fields. By reliably denoting the start and end of a structure with a standard, you help clients stay inside the structure, better guaranteeing they will not unintentionally miss a part when rounding out its substance.

Using Rules in Headers and Footers

An essential style way to deal with making archive families is to have a steady look and feel, including a standard header and footer for each record. Regularly, the header contains navigational devices that help clients effectively leap to interior segments just as related reports in the family, while the footer contains creator and record data just as criticism systems like an email connect to the website admin.

To guarantee that these headers and footers don't encroach on the fundamental archive substance, consider utilizing rules straightforwardly beneath the header or more the footer. By reliably separating your headers and footers utilizing rules, you assist clients with finding and center upon the fundamental body of your archive.

Inserting Images in Your Documents

Quite possibly the most convincing highlights of HTML and XHTML is their capacity to incorporate pictures with your archive text, either as an inborn segment of the report (inline pictures), as discrete records exceptionally chose for download through hyperlinks, or as a foundation for your report. When sensibly added to the body content, pictures - static and enlivened symbols, pictures, representations, drawings, etc. can make your archives more alluring, welcoming, and proficient looking, just as educational and simple to peruse. You may likewise uniquely empower a picture so it turns into a visual guide of hyperlinks. At the point when used to overabundance, notwithstanding, pictures make your report jumbled, confounding, and blocked off, just as pointlessly stretching the time it takes for clients to download and see your pages.

Understanding Image Formats

Neither HTML nor XHTML endorse an authority design for pictures. Be that as it may, the well-known programs explicitly oblige certain picture designs: GIF and JPEG, specifically (see following segments for clarifications). Most other sight and sound arrangements require extraordinary frill applications that every program proprietor should acquire, introduce, what's more, effectively work to see the unique records. So it's not very astounding that GIF and JPEG are the accepted picture guidelines on the Web.

Both picture designs were at that point in broad use before the Web appeared, so there's heaps of supporting programming out there to assist you with setting up your illustrations for one or the other organization. In any case, each has its own benefits and disadvantages, including highlights that a few programs misuse for uncommon showcase impacts.

GIF

The Graphics Interchange Format (GIF) was first created for picture move among clients of the CompuServe online assistance. The arrangement has a few highlights that make it mainstream for use in HTML and XHTML records. Its encoding is cross-stage, so that with proper GIF disentangling programming (included with most programs), the illustrations you make and make into a GIF record on a Macintosh, for instance, can be stacked into a Windows-based PC, decoded, and saw without a great deal of quarrel. The subsequent primary element is that GIF utilizes extraordinary pressure innovation that can fundamentally diminish the size of the picture document for quicker exchange over an organization. GIF pressure is "lossless," as well; none of a picture's unique information is changed or erased, so the uncompressed and decoded picture precisely coordinates with its unique. Also, GIF pictures can be handily enlivened.

Despite the fact that GIF picture documents perpetually have the .gif (or .GIF) filename postfix, there really are two GIF forms: the first GIF87 and an extended GIF89a, which upholds a few new highlights, including straightforward foundations, entwined capacity, and movement, that are mainstream with web creators. The right now mainstream programs support both GIF forms, which utilize the very encoding plan that maps 8-digit pixel esteems to a shading table, for a limit of 256 tones for every picture. Most GIF pictures have much less tones; there are unique apparatuses to work on the tones in more intricate illustrations. By improving on the GIF pictures, you make a more modest shading guide and upgrade pixel repetition for better record pressure and thus quicker downloading.

In any case, on account of the set number of shadings, a GIF-encoded picture isn't generally fitting, especially for photorealistic pictures. GIFs make superb symbols, diminished shading pictures, and drawings.

Since most graphical programs unequivocally support the GIF design, it is right now the most generally acknowledged picture encoding design on the Web. It is adequate for both inline pictures and remotely connected ones. If all else fails with respect to which picture arrangement to utilize, pick GIF. It will work in practically any circumstance. We can't avoid the impulse to call attention to that picky creators pick GIF.

Interlacing, transparency, and animation

GIF pictures can be made to perform three unique stunts: joining, straightforwardness, and activity. With entwining, a GIF picture apparently appears on the showcase, instead of dynamically streaming onto it start to finish. Regularly, a GIF encoded picture is a succession of pixel information, all together line by-column, start to finish of the picture. While the basic GIF picture renders onscreen like pulling down a window conceal, entwined GIFs open like a Venetian visually impaired. That is on the grounds that joining groupings each fourth column of the picture. Clients will see a full picture - start to finish, though fluffy - in a fourth of the time it takes to download and show the rest of the picture. The subsequent quarter-done picture as a rule is clear enough so clients with moderate organization associations can assess whether to set aside the effort to download the rest of the picture document.

Not every graphical program, albeit ready to show an intertwined GIF, are really ready to show the emerging impacts of interweaving. With those that do, clients actually can crush the impact by deciding to postpone picture show until after download and deciphering. More seasoned programs, then again, consistently download and unravel pictures before show and don't uphold the impact by any stretch of the imagination.

Another well-known impact accessible with GIF pictures - GIF89a-arranged pictures, really - is the capacity to make a segment of them straightforward so that what's under - generally the program window's experience - appears on the other side. The straightforward GIF picture has one tone in its shading map assigned as the foundation tone. The program basically overlooks any pixel in the picture that utilizes that foundation tone, along these lines letting the showcase window's experience appear on the other side. Via cautiously trimming its measurements and by utilizing a strong, adjacent foundation tone, a straightforward picture can be made to consistently merge into a page's encompassing substance or buoy above it.

Straightforward GIF pictures are incredible for any realistic you need to merge into the record and not stand apart as a rectangular square. Straightforward GIF logos are extremely mainstream, as are straightforward symbols and dingbats - any realistic that ought to seem to have a self-assertive, regular shape. You may likewise embed a straightforward picture in line with customary content to go about as an uncommon character glyph inside traditional content.

The drawback to straightforwardness is that the GIF picture will look inferior in the event that you don't eliminate its line when it is remembered for a hyperlink anchor (tag), or is usually exceptionally outlined. What's more, content stream occurs around the picture's rectangular measurements, not neighboring its clear shape. That can prompt pointlessly segregated pictures or odd-glancing segments in your site pages.

The third novel stunt accessible with GIF89a-organized pictures is the capacity to do basic edge by-outline activity. Utilizing unique GIF activity programming utilities, you may set up a solitary GIF89a document to contain a progression of GIF pictures. The program shows each picture in the record, consistently, something like the page-flipping liveliness booklets we had (even drew!) as children. Unique control fragments between each picture in the GIF record let you set the occasions the program goes through the total grouping (circling), how long to stop between each picture, regardless of whether the picture space gets cleaned to foundation before the program shows the following picture, etc. By consolidating these control highlights with those regularly accessible for

GIF pictures, including singular shading tables, straightforwardness, and intertwining, you can make some engaging and expand activities.

Basic GIF activity is amazing for one other significant explanation: you don't have to exceptionally program your HTML archives to accomplish liveliness. In any case, there is one significant disadvantage that restricts their utilization with the exception of little, symbol estimated, or slender groups of room in the program window: GIF movement records get huge quick, regardless of whether you are mindful so as not to rehash static bits of the picture in progressive activity cells. Furthermore, on the off chance that you have a few movements in a single archive, download deferrals may - and typically will - bother the client. In the event that there is any component that merits detailed examination for overabundance, it's GIF liveliness.

All GIF stunts - entwining, straightforwardness, and liveliness - don't simply occur; you need uncommon programming to set up the GIF record. Many picture instruments presently save your manifestations or procured pictures in GIF design, and most currently let you empower straightforwardness, just as allowed you to make entwined GIF records. There additionally are a large number of shareware and freeware programs particular for these errands, just as for making GIF liveliness. Investigate your #1 Internet programming documents for GIF designs and transformation devices.

JPEG

The Joint Photographic Experts Group (JPEG) is a norms body that created what is presently known as the JPEG picture encoding design. Like GIFs, JPEG pictures are stage free and uniquely compacted for rapid exchange through computerized correspondence innovations. Not at all like GIF, has JPEG upheld a huge number of colors for more itemized, photorealistic advanced pictures.

What's more, JPEG utilizes extraordinary calculations that yield a lot higher information pressure proportions. It isn't phenomenal, for instance, for a 200-kilobyte GIF picture to be decreased to a 30-kilobyte JPEG picture. To accomplish that stunning pressure, JPEG loses some picture information. Notwithstanding, you can change the level of "terribleness" with extraordinary JPEG instruments, so that albeit the uncompressed picture may not actually match the first, it will be close sufficient that the vast majority can't differentiate.

Despite the fact that JPEG is a great decision for photos, it is anything but an especially decent decision for representations. The calculations utilized for packing and uncompressing the picture leave recognizable curios when managing enormous regions of one tone. Thusly, in case you're attempting to show a drawing, the GIF configuration might be best.

The JPEG design, typically assigned by the .jpg (or .JPG) filename addition, is almost all around comprehended by the present graphical programs. On uncommon events, you'll run over a more seasoned program that can't straightforwardly show JPEG pictures.

When to Use Images

Most pictures merit 1,000 words. Yet, remember that nobody focuses on a windbag. As a matter of first importance, think about your report pictures as visual instruments, not unwarranted features. They should uphold your content substance and assist per users with exploring your records. Use pictures to explain, delineate, or epitomize the substance. Content-supporting photos, outlines, diagrams, guides, and drawings are on the whole characteristic and suitable competitors. Item photos are fundamental segments in online indexes and shopping guides, for instance. Also, interface empowered symbols and dingbats, including energized pictures, can be successful visual advisers for inward and outer assets. On the off chance that a picture doesn't do any of these important administrations for your archive, toss it out as of now!

Quite possibly the main contemplations when adding pictures to an archive is the extra postpone they add to the recovery time for a report over the organization, especially for modem associations. While a typical book archive may run, probably, 10 or 15 thousand bytes, pictures can undoubtedly reach out to a huge number of bytes each. What's more, the all-out recovery time for a record isn't simply equivalent to the amount of all its segment parts, yet in addition to intensified systems administration overhead postponements.

Contingent upon the speed of the association (transfer speed, typically communicated as pieces or bytes each second) also as organization clog that can postpone associations, a solitary report containing one 100-kilobyte picture may take anyplace from around 15 seconds through a 57.6 kilobit-per-second modem association before sunrise when most every other person is sleeping, to well more than ten minutes with a 9600 digit for every second modem around early afternoon. You get the image?

All things considered, obviously, pictures and other media are driving Internet suppliers to concoct quicker, better, heartier approaches to convey Web content. Before long, 57.6 kilobit-per-second modem associations will go the method of the pony and carriage (as 9600 piece for every subsequent modems as of now have), to be supplanted by advancements like link modems and ADSL. Surely, soon most associations will achieve information rates drawing nearer or surpassing what used to be accessible just to the greatest clients (other than costing a lot), over a megabit each second.

In any case, as the value brings down, use goes up, so there is the issue of clog. In the event that you are viewing for admittance to an overburdened worker, it doesn't make any difference how quick your association might be.

CHAPTER 3

When to Use Text

Text hasn't become dated. For certain clients, it is the lone bit of your archive they can get to. We contend that, by and large, your reports ought to be usable by per users who can't see pictures or have impaired their programmed download in their program to improve their association. While the inclination to add pictures to the entirety of your archives might be solid, there are times when unadulterated content reports bode well.

Reports being changed over to the Web from different arrangements seldom have implanted pictures. Reference materials and other genuine substance frequently is totally usable in a content just structure.

You ought to make text-possibly reports when access speed is basic. On the off chance that you realize that numerous clients will be competing for your pages, you ought to oblige them by dodging the utilization of pictures inside your records. In some limit cases, you may give a home (driving) page that allows per users to settle on copy assortments of your work: one containing the pictures, and another deprived of them. (The famous programs incorporate unique picture symbols as spot holders for yet-to-be downloaded pictures, which can waste and obfuscate your report's design into an indistinguishable wreck.)

Text is generally fitting - supporting pictures just, without decorations or superfluous illustrations - if your archives are to be promptly accessible by any of the many web ordering administrations. Pictures are quite often overlooked by these web indexes. In the event that the significant substance of your pages is furnished with pictures, almost no data about your records will discover its way into the online web indexes.

There are a few different ways to enhance the overhead and postpones inborn with pictures, other than being picky about which to remember for your reports:

Keep it basic

A full-screen, 24-bit shading realistic, in any event, when decreased in size by advanced pressure with one of the standard configurations like GIF or JPEG, is as yet going to be an organization data transfer capacity hoard. Obtain and utilize the different picture the executives' instruments to enhance picture measurements and number of shadings into the least number of pixels. Work on your drawings. Avoid all-encompassing photos. Stay away from enormous unfilled foundations in your pictures, just as needless lines and other space-burning-through components. Likewise abstain from vacillating (mixing two tones among neighboring pixels to accomplish a third tone); this procedure can altogether lessen the compressibility of your pictures. Make progress toward huge regions of uniform tones, which pack promptly in both GIF and JPEG design.

Reuse pictures

This is especially valid for symbols and GIF movements. Most programs reserve approaching record parts in neighborhood stockpiling for the actual motivation behind brisk, network association less recovery of information. For more modest GIF liveliness records, attempt to set up each progressive picture to refresh just bits that adjustment in the movement, instead of redraw the whole picture (this paces up the activity, as well).

Divide up large documents

This is an overall standard that incorporates pictures. Numerous little record portions, coordinated through hyperlinks (obviously!) and viable tables of substance will in general be preferred acknowledged by clients over a couple of huge reports. When all is said in done, individuals would prefer to "flip" a few pages than dillydally trusting that a huge one will download. (It's identified with the TV channel-riding disorder.) One acknowledged dependable guideline is to keep your records under 50 kilobytes each, so even the slowest associations will not excessively disappoint your per users.

Isolate necessarily large graphics

Give an uncommon connect to huge pictures, maybe one that incorporates a thumbnail of the realistic, subsequently allowing per users to choose if and when they need to invest the energy downloading the full picture. What's more, since the downloaded picture isn't blended in with other archive segments like inline pictures, it's a lot simpler for the per users to distinguish and save the picture on their framework's nearby stockpiling for later examination.

Specify image dimensions

At last, another approach to improve execution is by remembering the picture's rectangular tallness and width data for its tag. By providing those measurements, you kill the additional means the all-encompassing programs should take to download, analyze, and figure a picture's space in the archive. There is a disadvantage to this methodology, nonetheless, that we investigate later.

JPEG or GIF?

You may decide to utilize just JPEG or GIF pictures in your HTML records if your hotspots for pictures or your product toolset favors one over the other organization. Both are almost generally upheld by the present programs, so there shouldn't be any client seeing issues.

By the by, we prescribe that you get the offices to make and change over to the two organizations to exploit their extraordinary abilities. For example, utilize GIF's straightforwardness include for symbols and dingbats. On the other hand, use JPEG for enormous and brilliant pictures for quicker downloading.

The image Tag

The picture label allows you to reference and embed a realistic picture into the current content progression of your report. There is no inferred line or section break previously or after the picture tag, so pictures can be really "inline" with text and other substance.

The organization of the actual picture isn't characterized by the HTML or XHTML standard, albeit the famous graphical programs support GIF and JPEG pictures. The principles don't determine or limit the size or measurements of the picture, by the same token. Pictures may have quite a few tones, yet how those tones are delivered is profoundly program subordinate.

Picture introduction overall is very program explicit. Pictures might be disregarded by nongraphic programs. Programs working in an obliged climate may adjust the picture size or intricacy. Also, clients, especially those with moderate organization associations, may decide to concede picture stacking out and out. Likewise, you should ensure your records bode well and are helpful, regardless of whether the pictures are totally eliminated.

The src property

The src trait for the picture tag is required (except if you use dynsrc with Internet Explorer-based films. It worth is the picture record's URL, either supreme or comparative with the archive referring to the picture. To clean up their record stockpiling, creators normally gather picture documents into a different envelope they frequently name something like "pics" or "pictures.

The lowsrc quality

To the advantage of clients, especially those with moderate Internet associations, Netscape gives the lowsrc ally to the src characteristic in the image tag as an approach to accelerate archive delivering. The lowsrc characteristic's worth, as src, is the URL of a picture document that the program loads and shows when it first experiences the picture tag. At the point when the report has been totally stacked and can be perused by the client, Netscape recovers the picture determined by the src property.

The lowsrc picture is a low-goal, abridged rendition of the last src picture that heaps quicker by correlation with rapidly give per user a thought of its substance until the last, higher-goal picture ultimately replaces it onscreen. Be that as it may, the lowsrc trait can likewise be utilized for some extremely embellishments.

Netscape utilizes the lowsrc picture's measurements to save space in the record for both the lowsrc and src pictures, except if you expressly distribute that space with the tallness and width credits portrayed later in this part. Henceforth, if the components of the picture indicated in the src property are unique in relation to those for the lowsrc picture or your unequivocally included tallness and width esteems, the src picture will be decreased, augmented, extended, or compacted to fit in the distributed space. In addition, the lowsrc and src pictures needn't be indistinguishable, so you may exploit the deferred delivering of the src picture for basic movement.

The lowsrc quality is for Netscape as it were. Different programs disregard it and just burden the picture determined by the src characteristic. Netscape will not load either picture if the client decides not to auto-load pictures. All things considered, the two pictures will stack all together when the client taps the pictures catch or taps the picture symbol placeholder. No program stacks the lowsrc picture just; you should incorporate a src picture, in any case nothing will show up aside from the missing picture symbol.

The alt and longdesc attributes

The alt property determines elective content the program may show if picture show is unimaginable or crippled by the client. It's an alternative, yet one we energetically suggest you practice for most pictures in your report. Thusly, if the picture isn't accessible, the client actually has some sign of what it is that is absent.

Moreover, the most recent programs show the elective depiction in a content box when clients ignore their mouse the picture. As needs be, you may implant short, incidental data that springs up when clients ignore a little, inline symbol.

The incentive for the alt quality is a book line of up to 1024 characters on the off chance that you incorporate spaces or other accentuation. The string should be encased in quotes. The elective content may contain element references to uncommon characters, however it may not contain some other kind of markup; specifically, no style labels are permitted.

Graphical programs don't regularly show the alt property if the picture is accessible and the client has empowered picture downloading. Else, they embed the alt quality's content as a name close to a picture placeholder symbol. All around picked alt marks along these lines also support those clients with a graphical program who have crippled their programmed picture download as a result of a lethargic association with the Web.

Nongraphic, text-just programs like Lynx put the alt text straightforwardly into the substance stream very much like some other content component. Thus, when utilized adequately, the alt tag here and there can straightforwardly fill in for missing pictures. (You're content just program clients will value not being continually helped to remember their inferior web citizenship.) For model, consider utilizing a reference mark as the alt trait option in contrast to an extraordinary projectile symbol.

The longdesc quality is like the alt characteristic, yet considers bigger portrayals. The estimation of longdesc is the URL of a record containing a portrayal of the picture. On the off chance that you have a depiction longer than 1024 characters, utilize the longdesc characteristic to connection to it. Neither HTML 4 nor XHTML determine what the substance of the depiction should be, nor do any programs at present execute longdesc; what happens next is anyone's guess when concluding how to make those long portrayal.

The longdesc and align attribute

The norms don't characterize a default arrangement for pictures regarding other content and pictures in a similar line of text: you can't generally foresee how the content and pictures will look. HTML pictures regularly show up in accordance with a solitary line of text. Basic print media like magazines fold text over pictures, with a few lines close to and adjoining the picture, not simply a solitary line.

A large portion of the mainstream graphical programs embed a picture so its base lines up with the standard of the content - a similar arrangement determined by the characteristic estimation of base. In any case, report fashioners ought to expect that arrangement fluctuates among programs and consistently incorporate the ideal kind of picture arrangement.

Luckily, report originators can apply some command over the arrangement of pictures with the encompassing content through the adjust property for the picture tag. The HTML and XHTML norms determine five picture arrangement trait esteems: left, right, top, center, and base. The left and right qualities stream any ensuing content around the picture, which is moved to the relating edge; the leftover three adjust the picture vertically concerning the encompassing content. Netscape adds four more vertical arrangement ascribes to that rundown: text top, abs center, benchmark, and abs base, while Internet Explorer adds focus.

Top

The highest point of the picture is lined up with the top edge of the tallest thing in the current line of text. On the off chance that there could be no different pictures in the current line, the highest point of the picture is lined up with the highest point of the content.

Text top

The align text top trait and worth advises Netscape to adjust the highest point of the picture to the highest point of the tallest content thing in the current line. It is not the same as the top alternative, which adjusts the highest point of the picture to the highest point of the tallest thing, picture or text, in the current line. In the event that the line contains no different pictures that reach out over the highest point of the content, text top and top have a similar impact.

Abs middle

On the off chance that you set the adjust quality of the picture tag to abs center, the program will fit without a doubt the center of the picture to unquestionably the center of the current line. For Netscape and early forms of Internet Explorer, this is not quite the same as the basic center alternative, which adjusts the center of the picture to the standard of the current line of text (the lower part of the characters). Form 3 and later of Internet Explorer, then again, treat abs center equivalent to center and focus.

Centre

The middle picture arrangement esteem gets regarded equivalent to abs center by both Internet Explorer and Netscape, yet note that the programs treat abs center and center in an unexpected way.

Middle

Netscape and Internet Explorer treat the center picture arrangement esteem in an unexpected way: Netscape adjusts the center of the picture to the pattern of the content, paying little heed to other inline components. Web Explorer adjusts the center of the picture to the center of the tallest thing in the current line, text or picture. Notice the arrangements and contrasts, especially when just one picture contains the adjust quality.

Likewise note that Internet Explorer Version 3 and later treats center, abs center, and focus something similar, though prior Internet Explorer adaptations and Netscape recognize center and abs center arrangements.

Bottom and baseline (default)

With Netscape and early forms of Internet Explorer, the base and benchmark picture arrangement esteems have a similar impact as though you did exclude any arrangement characteristic whatsoever: the programs adjust the lower part of the picture in a similar flat plane as the standard of the content. This isn't to be mistaken for the abs base, which considers letter "descends" like the tail on the lowercase "y." Web Explorer Version 3 and later, then again, treat base equivalent to abs base.

Abs bottom

The align abs base characteristic advises the programs to adjust the lower part of the picture to the genuine lower part of the current line of text. The genuine base is the absolute bottom in the content considering descends, regardless of whether there are no descends in the line. A descend is the tail on a "y," for instance; the pattern of the content is the lower part of the "v" in the "y" character.

Utilize the top or center arrangement esteems for best combination of symbols, dingbats, or other uncommon inline impacts with the content substance. Something else, align=bottom (the default) generally gives the best appearance. While adjusting at least one pictures on a solitary line, select the arrangement that gives the best generally speaking appearance to your archive.

Wrapping text around images

The left and right picture arrangement esteems advise the program to put a picture against the left or right edge, individually, of the current content stream. The program at that point renders resulting report content in the leftover bit of the stream neighboring the picture. The net outcome is that the record content after the picture gets folded over the picture.

You can put pictures against the two edges all the while and the content will run down the center of the page between them. While text is streaming around a picture, the left (or right) edge of the page is briefly reclassified to be nearby the picture instead of the edge of the page. Ensuing pictures with a similar arrangement will pile facing one another. The accompanying source part accomplishes that amazed picture impact.

73

At the point when the content streams past the lower part of the picture, the edge gets back to its previous position, ordinarily at the edge of the program window.

Centering an image

Have you seen that you can't evenly focus a picture in the program window with the adjust property? The center and abs center qualities place the picture vertically with the current line, however the picture is evenly defended relying upon what substance precedes it in the current stream and the components of the program window.

You can evenly focus an inline picture in the program window, yet just if it's separated from encompassing substance, for example, by section, division, or line break labels. At that point, either utilize the middle tag, or utilize the adjust focus quality or focus defended style in the section or division tag to focus the picture.

Align is deprecated

The HTML 4 and XHTML guidelines have belittled the adjust characteristic for all labels, including picture, in respect to templates. In any case, the quality is extremely mainstream among HTML creators and stays very much upheld by the famous programs. In this way, while we do expect that sometime adjust will vanish, it will not be at any point in the near future. Simply don't say we didn't caution you.

The border attribute

Programs typically render pictures that likewise are hyperlinks (a picture remembered for a tag) with a two-pixel-wide shaded boundary, demonstrating to per user that the picture can be chosen to visit the related record. Utilize the boundary quality and a pixel-width thickness worth to eliminate (line 0) or enlarge that picture line. Be mindful that this characteristic, as well, is expostulated in HTML 4 and XHTML in lieu of templates, however keeps on being very much upheld by the mainstream programs.

Removing the image border

You can kill the line around a picture hyperlink by and large with the border=0 trait inside the picture tag. For certain pictures, especially picture maps, the shortfall of a line can improve the presence of your pages. Pictures that are obviously connect catches to different pages may likewise look best without a line.

Be cautious, however, that by eliminating the boundary, you don't reduce your page's convenience. No boundary implies you've eliminated a typical visual marker of a connection, making it less simple for users to discover the connections on the page. Programs will change the mouse cursor as per users ignore it a picture that is a hyperlink, yet you ought not to accept they will, nor should you make per users test your borderless pictures to discover covered up joins.

We firmly suggest that you utilize some extra route with borderless pictures to tell your users to tap the pictures. In any event, including basic content guidelines will go far to making your pages more open to per users.

The height and width attributes

At any point watch the presentation of a page's substance move around inconsistently while the report is stacking? That happens in light of the fact that the program straightens out the page design to oblige each stacked picture. The program decides the size of a picture and, consequently, the rectangular space to save for it in the presentation window, by recovering the picture record and extricating its implanted stature and width details. The program at that point changes the page's showcase format to embed that image in the display. This isn't the most effective approach to deliver a report, since the program should consecutively inspect each picture record and ascertain its screen space prior to delivering adjoining and resulting archive content. That can essentially build the measure of time it takes to deliver the archive and upset perusing by the client.

Another update that pictures are discrete records, which are stacked separately and notwithstanding the source report.

A more effective path for creators to indicate a picture's measurements is with the stature and width picture credits. That way, the program can hold space before really downloading a picture, speeding archive delivering and taking out the substance moving. The two ascribes require a whole number worth that demonstrates the picture size in pixels; and the request wherein they show up in the picture tag isn't significant.

Resizing and flood-filling images
A secret component of the stature and width credits is that you don't have to determine the genuine picture measurements; the characteristic qualities can be bigger or more modest than the real size of the picture. The program naturally scales the picture to fit the predefined space. This gives you a ready to take care of business method of making thumbnail adaptations of huge pictures and an approach to augment little pictures. Be cautious, however: the program actually should download the whole document, regardless of what its last delivered size is, and you will contort a picture in the event that you don't hold its unique tallness versus width extents.

Another stunt with stature and width gives a simple method to flood-fill regions of your page and can likewise improve report execution. Assume you need to embed a hued bar across your record.

Instead of make a picture to the full measurements, make one that is only one pixel high and wide and set it to the ideal tone. At that point utilize the stature and width ascribes to scale it to the bigger size.

One final stunt with the width quality is to utilize a rate esteem rather than a flat out pixel esteem. This makes the program scale the picture to a level of the archive window width. Along these lines, to make a hued bar 20 pixels high and the width of the window, you could utilize.

As the record window changes size, the picture will change size too.

In the event that you give a rate width and preclude the tallness, the program will hold the picture's viewpoint proportion as it develops and shrivels. This implies that the stature will consistently be in the right extent to the width and the picture will show without mutilation.

Problems with height and width

Albeit the tallness and width credits for the picture tag can improve execution and let you perform slick stunts, there is a knotty disadvantage to utilizing them. The program puts to the side the predetermined square shape of room to the endorsed measurements in the presentation window regardless of whether the client has killed programmed download of pictures. What the client regularly is left with is a page brimming with semi-void casings with inane picture placeholder symbols inside. The page looks frightfully incomplete and is for the most part pointless. Without going with measurements, then again, the program basically embeds a placeholder symbol in line with the encompassing content, so in any event there's something there to peruse in the presentation.

We don't have a response to this predicament, other than to demand that you utilize the alt trait with some engaging content so clients in any event understand what they are absent. We do suggest that you incorporate these size credits since we energize any training that improves network execution.

The hspace and vspace attributes

Graphical programs as a rule don't give you much space between a picture and the content around it. Also, except if you make a straightforward picture line that grows the space between them, the ordinary two-pixel support between a picture and adjoining text is simply excessively close for most creators' solace. Add the picture into a hyperlink, and the unique shaded boundary will invalidate any straightforward cushion space you worked to make, just as cause much more to notice how close the contiguous content knocks into the picture.

The hspace and vspace characteristics can give your pictures space to breathe. With hspace, you indicate the quantity of pixels of additional room to leave between the picture and text on the left and right sides of the picture; the vspace esteem is the quantity of pixels on the top and base.

We're certain you'll concur that the extra space around the picture makes the content simpler to peruse and the general page more alluring.

The ismap and usemap attributes

The ismap and usemap ascribes for the picture label tell the program that the picture is a unique mouse-selectable visual guide of at least one hyperlinks, ordinarily known as a picture map. The ismap style of picture maps, known as a worker side picture map, might be determined distinctly inside a label hyperlink.

The program naturally sends the x, y position of the mouse (comparative with the upper-left corner of the picture) to the worker when the client clicks some place on the ismap picture. Exceptional worker programming may then utilize those directions to decide a reaction.

The usemap property gives a customer side picture map instrument that adequately takes out worker side preparing of the mouse directions and its officeholder network deferrals and issues. Utilizing uncommon guide and territory labels, HTML creators give a guide of directions to the hyperlink-touchy locales in the usemap picture alongside related hyperlink URLs. The estimation of the usemap quality is a URL that focuses to that uncommon map section. The program on the client's PC deciphers the directions of a tick of the mouse on the picture into some activity, including stacking and showing another report.

For instance, the accompanying source exceptionally encodes the 100 x 100-pixel map2.gif picture into four sections, every one of which, whenever clicked by the client, connections to an alternate archive. Notice we've included, truly, the ismap picture map preparing ability in the model image tag with the goal that clients of other, usemap-inadequate programs approach the other option, worker side system to handle the picture map.

Topographical guides make amazing ismap and usemap models: perusing a cross country organization's pages, for example, the clients may tap on the places where they grew up on a guide to get the locations and telephone numbers for close by retail outlets. The benefit of the usemap customer side picture map preparing is that it doesn't need a worker or exceptional worker programming thus, dissimilar to the ismap component, can be utilized in non-web (network less) conditions, like nearby records.

The class, dir, occasion, id, lang, style, and title attribute

A few almost widespread credits give you a typical method to distinguish (title) and name (id) the picture label's substance for later reference or robotized treatment, to change the substance's showcase attributes (class, style), and to reference the language (lang) utilized and related heading the content should stream (dir). Furthermore, obviously, there are for the most part the client occasions that may occur in and around the labeled substance that the program faculties and that you may respond to through an on-occasion characteristic and some programming.

Of these numerous HTML 4 and XHTML ascribes, id is the most significant. It allows you to name the picture for later access by a program or program activity.

The excess ascribes have sketchy significance in setting with picture. Without a doubt, there are a couple of template alternatives accessible that may impact a picture's showcase, and a title is a great idea to incorporate, in spite of the fact that alt is better. What's more, it's difficult to envision what the impact of language (lang) or its introduction course (dir) might have on an picture.

Video Extensions

The extraordinary controls, dynsrc, circle, and start trait expansions for the img tag are exceptional to Internet Explorer and are not HTML 4 or XHTML standard ascribes. They let you implant an inline film into the body content, very much like a picture.

Identical conduct is accessible in Netscape through an expansion program known as a module. Modules place an extra weight on the client, in that every client should discover and introduce the suitable module prior to having the option to see the inline video. The Internet Explorer picture label expansions, then again, make video show an inborn piece of the program.

Notwithstanding, the Internet Explorer film augmentations right now are extremely restricted. They are not upheld by some other program and can be utilized uniquely with Audio Video Interleave (AVI) designed film records, since that is the player design incorporated into Internet Explorer and empowered through Microsoft's Windows working framework programming. In addition, ongoing developments in program innovation, articles, and applets specifically may make Internet Explorer's methodology of expanding the all-around over-burden picture label old.

The dynsrc trait

Utilize the dynsrc trait augmentation in the img tag to reference an AVI film for inline show by Internet Explorer. Its necessary worth is the URL of the film record encased in quotes. For instance, this content shows the tag and characteristic for an AVI film record.

The program puts to the side a video viewport in the HTML show window and plays the film, with sound if it's remembered for the clasp and if PC can play sound. Web Explorer treats dynsrc motion pictures like inline pictures: in accordance with current body substance and as per the component of the video outline. Also, as normal pictures, the dynsrc referred to film record gets shown following download from the worker. You may change those defaults and add some client controls with different credits, as depicted later.

Since any remaining programs as of now disregard the uncommon Internet Explorer credits for films, they may get befuddled by a picture label that doesn't contain the usually required src characteristic and a picture URL. We suggest that you incorporate the src quality and a substantial picture document URL taking all things together picture labels, including those that reference a film for Internet Explorer clients. Different programs show the actually picture instead of the film; Internet Explorer does the opposite and plays the film, yet doesn't show the picture. Note that the request for credits doesn't make any difference.

Web Explorer loads and plays the AVI film intro.avi; other graphical programs will load and show the mvstill.gif picture all things considered.

Conclusion

Our objective recorded as a hard copy this book is to help you become conversant in HTML and XHTML, completely knowledgeable in their punctuation, semantics, and components of style. We adopt the regular learning strategy, utilizing models: great ones, obviously.

We cover each component of the presently acknowledged adaptations (HTML 4.01 and XHTML 1.0) of the dialects in detail, just as the entirety of the current expansions upheld by the mainstream programs, clarifying how every component works and how it interfaces with the wide range of various components.

All through the book we will give your ideas for style and arrangement to assist you with choosing how best to utilize HTML and XHTML to achieve an assortment of assignments, from straightforward online documentation to complex advertising and deals introductions. We'll show you what works and what doesn't, what sounds good to the individuals who see your pages, and what may be befuddling.

To put it plainly, this book is a finished manual for making reports utilizing HTML and XHTML, beginning with essential punctuation and semantics, and getting done with wide style rules to assist you with making delightful, educational, open archives that you'll be glad to convey to your programs.

HTML PROGRAMMING

A Complete Step-by-step Guide to HTML to Master Your Web Designing And More..

By John Davis

The trademarks used are without any consent, and the publication of the trademark is without permission or backing by the trademark owner. All trademarks and brands within this book are for clarifying purposes only and are owned by the owners themselves s, not affiliated with this document.

As yet, we've managed HTML and XHTML reports as independent elements, focusing on the language components you use for structure and to arrange your work. The genuine force of these markup dialects, notwithstanding, lies in their capacity to combine assortments of records into a full library of data and to connect your library of reports with different assortments all throughout the planet. Similarly as per users have extensive authority over how the record looks onscreen, with hyperlinks they additionally have power over the request for introduction as they explore through your data. It's the "HT" in HTML and XHTML - hypertext - and the contort turns the Web.

1.1 Hypertext Basics

A basic element of hypertext is that you can hyperlink reports; you can highlight somewhere else inside the current archive, inside another record in the nearby assortment, or inside a report anyplace on the Internet. The archives become an unpredictably woven snare of data. (Get the name similarity now?) The target record is typically some way or another identified with and improves the source; the connecting component in the source ought to pass on that relationship to the user.

Hyperlinks can be utilized for a wide range of impacts. They can be utilized inside tables of substance and arrangements of points. With a tick of the mouse on their program screen or a press of a key on their console, per users select and naturally leap to a subject of interest in a similar archive or to another record situated in an altogether distinctive assortment somewhere near the world.

Hyperlinks additionally direct per users toward more data about a referenced subject. "For more data, see Kumquats on Parade," for instance. Creators use hyperlinks to lessen redundant data. For example, we prescribe you sign your name to every one of your records. Instead of incorporate full contact data in each archive, a hyperlink associates your name to a solitary spot that contains your location, telephone number, etc.

A hyperlink, or anchor in standard speech, is set apart by the tag and comes in two flavors. As we depict in detail later, one kind of anchor makes a problem area in the report that, when initiated and chosen (as a rule with a mouse) by the client, makes the program connect. It consequently loads and shows another segment of something similar or another report inside and out, or triggers some Internet administration related activity, like sending email or downloading an uncommon record. The other sort of anchor makes a name, a spot in a report that can be referred to as a hyperlink.

The two sorts of anchors utilize a similar tag; maybe that is the reason they have a similar name. We think that its simpler in the event that you separate them and think about the one kind that gives the area of interest and address of a hyperlink as the "connect," and the other sort that denotes the objective bit of an archive as the "anchor."

There likewise are some mouse-related occasions related with hyperlinks, which, through JavaScript, let you consolidate some energizing impacts.

1.2 Referencing Documents: The URL

As we examined before, each archive on the World Wide Web has a remarkable location. (Envision the disarray on the off chance that they didn't.) The record's location is known as its uniform asset finder (URL). "URL" typically is articulated "you are ell," not "baron."

A few labels incorporate a URL quality worth, including hyperlinks, inline pictures, and structures. All utilization a similar URL linguistic structure to determine the area of a web asset, paying little mind to the sort or substance of that asset. That is the reason it's known as a uniform asset finder.

Since they can be utilized to address practically any asset on the Internet, URLs arrive in an assortment of flavors. All URLs, be that as it may, have a similar high level sentence structure.

The plan depicts the sort of item the URL references is, all things considered, and the part that is exceptional to the particular plan. The significant thing to note is that the plan is constantly isolated from the plan by a colon with no interceding spaces.

Compose URLs utilizing the displayable characters in the US-ASCII character set. For instance, definitely you have heard what has gotten annoyingly basic on the radio for a declared business site.

On the off chance that you need to utilize a character in a URL that isn't essential for this character set, you should encode the character utilizing an extraordinary documentation. The encoding documentation replaces the ideal character with three characters: a percent sign and two hexadecimal digits whose worth relates to the situation of the character in the ASCII character set.

This is simpler than it sounds. Perhaps the most widely recognized exceptional characters is the space (Macintosh proprietors, take unique notification), whose position in the character set is 20 hexadecimal. You can't type a space in a URL (indeed, you can, yet it will not work). Or maybe, supplant spaces in the URL with %20.

This URL really recovers a record named new estimating html from the worker.

Notwithstanding the nonprinting characters, you'll need to encode saved and dangerous characters in your URLs also.

Saved characters are those that include a particular significance inside the actual URL. For instance, the slice character isolates components of a pathname inside a URL. On the off chance that you need to remember a slice for a URL that isn't proposed to be a component separator, you'll need to encode it as %2F.

Hexadecimal numbering depends on 16 characters: through 9 finished by A F, which in decimal are identical to values through 15. Likewise, letter case for these all-encompassing qualities isn't critical; "a" (10 decimal) is equivalent to "A".

This URL really references the asset named register on the worker and passes the string 3/4 to it, as depicted by the question mark (?). Probably, the asset is a worker side program that plays out some number-crunching capacity on the passed worth and returns an outcome.

Dangerous characters are those that include no uncommon significance inside the URL, yet may have an exceptional importance in the setting where the URL is composed. For instance, twofold statements ("") delimit URL quality qualities in labels. If you somehow happened to incorporate a twofold quote straightforwardly in a URL, you would likely befuddle the program. All things being equal, you ought to encode the twofold quote as %22 to dodge any conceivable clash.

When all is said in done, you ought to consistently encode a character if there is some uncertainty concerning whether it tends to be set as-is in a URL. As a dependable guideline, any character other than a letter, number, or any of the characters ought to be encoded.

It is never a mistake to encode a character, except if that character has a particular importance in the URL. For instance, encoding the slices in an http URL makes them be utilized as customary characters, not as pathname delimiters, breaking the URL.

2.2 The http URL

The http URL is by a wide margin the most well-known inside the World Wide Web. It is utilized to get to archives from a web worker, and it has two organizations:

A portion of the parts are discretionary. Truth be told, the most well-known type of the http URL is basically similar to this, which assigns

the one of a kind worker and the registry way and name of a record.

2.3 The http server

The worker is the novel Internet name or Internet Protocol (IP) mathematical location of the PC framework that stores the web asset. We speculate you'll generally utilize all the more effortlessly recalled Internet names for the workers in your URLs.

Every Internet-associated PC has a novel location, a numeric (IP) address, obviously, in light of the fact that PCs bargain just in numbers. People incline toward names, so the Internet people give us an assortment of unique workers and programming (Domain Name System or DNS) that consequently resolve Internet names into IP addresses.

InterNIC, a not-for-profit office, registers area names generally on an early bird gets the worm premise, and appropriates new names to DNS workers around the world.

The name comprises of a few sections, including the worker's genuine name and the progressive names of its organization space, each part isolated by a period.

The three-letter postfix of the area name distinguishes the sort of association or business that works that segment of the Internet. For example, "com" is a business endeavor; "edu" is a scholastic establishment; and "gov" distinguishes an administration based space. Outside the United States, a less-spellbinding postfix is frequently allocated, normally a two-letter truncation of the nation name, for example, "jp" for Japan and "de" for Deutschland. Numerous associations all throughout the planet currently utilize the nonexclusive three-letter postfixes instead of the more traditional two-letter public additions.

It has become something of a show that website admins name their workers www for brisk and simple recognizable proof on the Web. For example, a web worker's name is www, which, alongside the distributer's space name, turns into the effortlessly recollected site. Additionally, Sun Microsystems' web worker is named www.sun.com; Apple Computer's is www.apple.com, and even Microsoft makes their web worker effectively important as www.microsoft.com. The naming show has exceptionally clear advantages, which you, as well, should exploit on the off chance that you are called upon to make a web worker for your association.

You may likewise determine the location of a worker utilizing its mathematical IP address. The location is a grouping of four numbers, zero to 255, isolated by periods. Substantial IP addresses.

It'd be a dull redirection to mention to you know what the numbers mean or how to get an IP address from a space name, especially since you'll only very seldom utilize one of every a URL. Or maybe, this is a decent spot to hyperlink: get any great Internet organizing composition for thorough detail on IP tending to.

2.4 The http port

The port is the quantity of the correspondence port to which the customer program interfaces with the worker. It's a systems administration thing: workers perform numerous capacities other than present web records and assets to customer programs: electronic mail, FTP report brings, file system sharing, etc. Albeit all that network movement may come into the worker on a solitary wire, it's commonly isolated into programming overseen "ports" for administration explicit interchanges - something practically equivalent to boxes at your neighborhood mail center.

The default URL port for web workers is 80. Exceptional secure web workers (Secure HTTP, SHTTP or Secure Socket Layer, SSL) run on port 443. Most web workers today utilize port 80; you need to incorporate a port number alongside a promptly going before colon in your URL if the objective worker doesn't utilize port 80 for web correspondence.

At the point when the Web was in its earliest stages, pioneer website admins ran their Wild Web associations on a wide range of port numbers. For specialized and security reasons, framework chairman advantages are needed to introduce a worker on port 80. Lacking such advantages, these website admins picked other, all the more effectively open, port numbers.

Presently that web workers have gotten satisfactory and are under the consideration and taking care of capable managers, archives being served on some port other than 80 or 443 should make you keep thinking about whether that worker is truly alright. Doubtlessly, the dissident worker is being controlled by a smart client unbeknownst to the worker's true blue framework directors.

2.5 The http path

The archive way is the Unix-style progressive area of the document in the worker's stockpiling framework. The pathname comprises of at least one names isolated by cuts. Everything except the last name address catalogs driving down to the report; the last name is normally that of the actual record.

It has become a show that for simple recognizable proof, HTML record names end with the addition .html (otherwise they're plain ASCII text documents, recollect?). Albeit ongoing forms of Windows permit longer postfixes, their clients regularly adhere to the three-letter .htm name addition for HTML records.

Albeit the worker name in a URL isn't case-delicate, the archive pathname might be. Since most web workers are run on Unix-based frameworks and UNIX record names are case-delicate, the archive pathname will be case-touchy, as well. Web workers running on Windows machines are not case-touchy, so the record pathname is not, however since it is difficult to know the working arrangement of the worker you are getting to, consistently expect that the worker has case-touchy pathnames and take care to get the case right when composing your URLs.

Certain shows with respect to the record pathname have emerged. In the event that the last component of the archive way is a catalog, not a solitary record, the worker generally will send back either a posting of the registry substance or the HTML file report in that index. You should end the report name for an index with a following cut character, yet practically speaking, most workers will respect the solicitation regardless of whether the character is excluded.

In the event that the catalog name is only a cut alone or some of the time nothing by any stretch of the imagination, you will recover the main (high level) report or purported landing page in the highest root index of the worker. Each all-around planned http worker ought to have an alluring, very much planned "landing page"; it's a shorthand route for clients to get to your web assortment since they don't have to recall the report's real filename, simply your worker's name.

Another bend: if the main part of the record way begins with the tilde character (~), it implies that the remainder of the pathname starts from the individual registry in the home catalog of the predefined client on the worker machine. For example, the URL http://www.kumquat.com/~chuck/would recover the high level page from Chuck's record assortment.

Various workers have various methods of finding reports inside a client's home catalog. Many quest for the archives in a catalog named public_html. Unix-based workers are partial to the name index.html for home pages. At the point when all else comes up short, workers will in general hack up the main content report in the landing page catalog.

2.6 The http document fragment

The part is an identifier that focuses to a particular segment of an archive. In URL particulars, it follows the worker and pathname and is isolated by the pound sign (#). A section identifier demonstrates to the program that it should start showing the objective record at the demonstrated part name. As we depict in more detail later in this section, you embed piece names into a record either with the widespread id label quality or with the name characteristic for a tag. Like pathnames, a section name might be any grouping of characters.

The section name and the previous hash image are discretionary; overlook them while referring to a record without characterized pieces.

Officially, the piece component just applies to HTML or XHTML archives. On the off chance that the objective of the URL is some other archive type, the piece name might be misconstrued by the program.

Pieces are valuable for long archives. By recognizing key areas of your report with a part name, you make it simple for per users to connect straightforwardly to that segment of the archive, maintaining a strategic distance from the monotony of looking over or looking through the record to get to the segment that intrigues them.

As a general guideline, we suggest that each part header in your archives be joined by a comparable section name. By reliably observing this standard, you'll make it feasible for per users to leap to any segment in any of your records. Parts likewise make it simpler to construct tables of substance for your record families.

2.7 The http search parameter

The pursuit part of the http URL, alongside its previous question mark, is discretionary. It shows that the way is an accessible or executable asset on the worker. The substance of the pursuit segment is passed to the worker as boundaries that control the hunt or execution work.

The genuine encoding of boundaries in the inquiry segment is reliant upon the worker and the asset being referred to. The boundaries for accessible assets are shrouded later in this part, when we talk about accessible reports. Boundaries for executable assets are talked about later.

Despite the fact that our underlying introduction of http URLs demonstrated that a URL can have either a part identifier or an inquiry segment, a few programs let you utilize both in a solitary URL. On the off chance that you so want, you can follow the pursuit boundary with a section identifier, advising the program to start showing the aftereffects of the inquiry at the demonstrated part. Netscape, for instance, upholds this utilization.

We don't suggest this sort of URL, however. As a matter of first importance, it doesn't deal with a great deal of programs. Comparably significant, utilizing a section infers that you are certain that the aftereffects of the pursuit will have a piece of that name characterized inside the report. For enormous report assortments, this is not really likely. You are in an ideal situation precluding the part, showing the list items from the start of the report, and maintaining a strategic distance from possible disarray among your per users.

The JavaScript URL really is a pseudo-convention, not generally remembered for conversations of URLs. However, with cutting edge programs like Netscape and Internet Explorer, the JavaScript URL can be related with a hyperlink and used to execute JavaScript orders when the client chooses the connection.

3.1 The JavaScript URL arguments

What follows the JavaScript pseudo-convention is at least one semicolon-isolated JavaScript articulations and strategies, including references to multi-articulation JavaScript capacities that you insert inside the script tag in your reports.

The main model contains a solitary JavaScript strategy that actuates a ready exchange with the straightforward message.

The second JavaScript URL model contains two contentions: the primary calls a JavaScript work, doFlash, which apparently you have found somewhere else in the archive inside the content tag and which maybe streaks the foundation shade of the report window between the red and blue. The subsequent articulation is a similar ready strategy as in the primary model, with a somewhat extraordinary message.

The JavaScript URL may show up in a hyperlink sans contentions, as well. All things considered, the Netscape program alone - not Internet Explorer - opens an exceptional JavaScript supervisor wherein the client may type in and test the different articulations and strategies.

Chapter 4. The ftp URL

The ftp URL is utilized to recover archives from a FTP (File Transfer Protocol) worker.

FTP is an old Internet convention that traces all the way back to the Dark Ages, around 1975. It was planned as a basic method to move records among machines and is well known and helpful right up 'til the present time. A few group who can't run a genuine web worker will put their records on a worker that speaks FTP all things considered.

4.1 The ftp user and password

FTP is a validated help, implying that you should have a substantial username and secret phrase to recover archives from a worker. Nonetheless, most FTP workers additionally support confined, non-validated admittance known as mysterious FTP. In this mode, anybody can supply the username "mysterious" and be allowed admittance to a restricted segment of the worker's reports. Most FTP workers additionally accept (yet may not concede) unknown access if the username and secret word are discarded.

On the off chance that you are utilizing a ftp URL to get to a site that requires a username and secret phrase, remember the client and secret key parts for the URL, alongside the colon (:) and "at" sign (@). All the more regularly, you'll be getting to a mysterious FTP worker, and the client and secret phrase segments can be discarded.

104

In the event that you keep the client segment alongside the "at" sign, however overlook the secret word and the previous colon, most programs will provoke you for a secret word subsequent to associating with the FTP worker. This is the suggested method of getting to confirmed assets on a FTP worker; it keeps others from seeing your password.

We suggest you never place a ftp URL with a username and secret key in any HTML archive. The thinking is basic: anybody can recover the record, separate the username and secret phrase from the URL, sign into the FTP worker, and alter its archives.

4.2 The ftp server and port

The ftp worker and port are limited by similar standards as the worker and port in a http URL, as portrayed previously. The worker should be a substantial Internet area name or IP address of a FTP worker. The port indicates the port on which the worker is tuning in for demands.

On the off chance that the port and its previous colon are overlooked, the default port of 21 is utilized. It is important to determine the port just if the FTP worker is running on some port other than 21.

4.3 The ftp path and transfer type

The way segment addresses a progression of indexes, isolated by slices prompting the document to be recovered. As a matter of course, the record is recovered as a double document; this can be changed by adding the typecode (and the former ;type=) to the URL.

In the event that the typecode is set to d, the way is thought to be an index. The program will demand a posting of the index substance from the worker and show this leaning to the client. On the off chance that the typecode is some other letter, it is utilized as a boundary to the FTP type order prior to recovering the record referred to by the way. While some FTP workers may execute different codes, most workers acknowledge (i) to start a paired exchange and (a) to regard the record as a flood of ASCII text.

Chapter 5. The file URL

The record URL determines a document put away on a machine without showing the convention used to recover the document. Thusly, it has restricted use in an organized climate. Its genuine advantage, in any case, is that it can reference a record on the client's machine, and is especially helpful for referring to individual HTML report assortments, like those "under development" and not yet prepared for general dissemination, or HTML archive assortments.

5.1 The file server

The record worker, similar to the http worker depicted before, should be the Internet area name or IP address of the machine containing the document to be recovered. No suppositions are made with respect to how the program may contact the machine to acquire the document; apparently the program can make some association, maybe by means of a Network File System or FTP, to get the record.

On the off chance that the worker is discarded, or the exceptional name local host is utilized, the record is expected to live on a similar machine whereupon the program is running. For this situation, the program essentially gets to the document utilizing the ordinary offices of the nearby working framework. Indeed, this is the most widely recognized use of the document URL. By making archive families on a diskette and referring to your hyperlinks you make a distributable, independent record assortment that doesn't need an organization association with use.

5.2 The file path

This is the way of the record to be recovered on the ideal worker. The sentence structure of the way may vary dependent on the working arrangement of the worker; make certain to encode any possibly perilous characters in the way.

Chapter 6. The news URL

The news URL gets to either a solitary message or a whole newsgroup inside the Usenet news framework.

A heartbreaking restriction in news URLs is that they don't permit you to determine a worker for the newsgroup. Or maybe, clients indicate their news-worker asset in their program inclinations. At one time, not long prior, Internet newsgroups were almost generally disseminated; all news workers conveyed all the equivalent newsgroups and their particular articles, so one news worker was on par with any. Today, the sheer heft of plate space expected to store the day by day volume of newsgroup action is regularly restrictive for any single news worker, and there's likewise nearby oversight of newsgroups. Consequently you can't expect that all newsgroups, and positively not all articles for a specific newsgroup, will be accessible on the client's news worker.

Numerous clients' programs may not be accurately arranged to understand news. We suggest you try not to put news URLs in your reports besides in uncommon cases.

6.1 Accessing entire newsgroups

There are a few thousand newsgroups gave to essentially every possible point under the sun and past. Each gathering has a remarkable name, made out of various leveled components isolated by periods.

6.2 Accessing single messages

Each message on a news worker has a one of a kind message identifier (ID) related with it. The unique_string is an arrangement of ASCII characters; the worker is generally the name of the machine from which the message started. The unique_string should be interesting among every one of the messages that started from the worker.

When all is said in done, message IDs are enigmatic groupings of characters not promptly comprehended by people. Besides, the life expectancy of a message on a worker is normally estimated in days, after which the message is erased and the message ID is not, at this point substantial. The main concern: single message news URLs are hard to make, become invalid rapidly, and are for the most part not utilized.

Chapter 7. The nntp URL

The nntp URL goes past the news URL to give a total instrument to getting to articles in the Usenet news framework.

7.1 The nntp server and port

The nntp worker and port are characterized likewise to the http worker and port, portrayed prior. The worker should be the Internet space name or IP address of a nntp worker; the port is the port on which that worker is tuning in for demands. In the event that the port and its former colony are excluded, the default port of 119 is utilized.

7.2 The nntp newsgroup and article

The newsgroup is the name of the gathering from which an article is to be recovered.

The article is the numeric id of the ideal article inside that newsgroup. Albeit the article number is simpler to decide than a message id, it falls prey to similar constraints of single message references utilizing the news URL. In particular, articles don't keep going long on most nntp workers, and nntp URLs immediately become invalid thus.

Most programs open an email arrangement window when the client chooses a mailto URL. The beneficiary's location is filled in, taken from the URL, however the message subject and different other header fields are left clear. Numerous website admins might want to fill in these fields as a graciousness to their users, yet the URL standard gives no real way to do this.

The advanced programs stretch out the mailto URL to fill this hole. By adding CGI-like boundaries to the mailto header, you can set the estimation of the subject with Netscape and Internet Explorer, and furthermore cc (duplicate) and bcc (daze duplicate) fields for the mail message with Netscape. These URLs work with Netscape; just the first works effectively with Internet Explorer.

As you can most likely speculation, the principal URL sets the subject of the message. Note that spaces are permitted; you don't need to supplant them with the hexadecimal identical %20. Also, the last model sets the bcc field of the message. You may likewise set a few fields in a single URL by isolating the field definitions with ampersands.

Web Explorer Version 3 doesn't perceive the bcc and cc fields in the mailto URL and will either whine about them on the off chance that they show up alone or attach them to a first subject.

The telnet URL opens an intelligent meeting with an ideal worker, permitting the client to sign in and utilize the machine. Frequently, the association with the machine naturally begins a particular assistance for the client; in different cases, the client should realize the orders to type to utilize the framework.

9.1 The telnet user and password

The telnet client and secret word are utilized precisely like the client and secret phrase parts of the ftp URL, portrayed already. Specifically, similar provisos apply in regards to securing your secret phrase and never putting it inside a URL.

Actually like the ftp URL, in the event that you preclude the secret key from the URL, the program should incite you for a secret word not long prior to reaching the telnet worker.

In the event that you discard both the client and secret phrase, the telnet happens without providing a client name. For certain workers, telnet consequently associates with a default administration when no username is provided. For other people, the program may incite for a username and secret phrase when making the association with the telnet worker.

9.2 The telnet server and port

The telnet worker and port are characterized comparatively to the http worker and port, portrayed previously. The worker should be the Internet area name or IP address of a telnet worker; the port is the port on which that worker is tuning in for demands. On the off chance that the port and its first colon are overlooked, the default port of 23 is utilized.

Chapter 10. The gopher URL

Gopher is a web-like report recovery framework that accomplished some prevalence on the Internet not long before the World Wide Web took off, making Gopher old. Some Gopher workers actually exist, however, and the gopher URL allows you to get to Gopher records.

10.1 The gopher server and port

The gopher worker and port are characterized comparatively to the http worker and port, portrayed already. The worker should be the Internet space name or IP address of a gopher worker; the port is the port on which that worker is tuning in for demands.

On the off chance that the port and its previous colon are overlooked, the default port of 70 is utilized.

10.2 The gopher path

The sort is a solitary character esteem signifying the kind of the gopher asset. On the off chance that the whole way is discarded from the gopher URL, the sort defaults to 1.

The selector relates to the way of an asset on the Gopher worker. It very well might be discarded, in which case the high level list of the Gopher worker is recovered.

In the event that the Gopher asset is really a Gopher web search tool, the pursuit part gives the string to which to look. The inquiry string should be gone before by an encoded flat tab (%09).

In the event that the Gopher worker upholds Gopher+ assets, the gopherplus segment supplies the important data to find that asset. The specific substance of this part shifts dependent on the assets on the gopher worker. This segment is gone before by an encoded flat tab (%09). In the event that you need to incorporate the gopherplus part however exclude the hunt segment, you should in any case supply both encoded tabs inside the URL.

You may compose a URL in one of two different ways: total or relative. An outright URL is the finished location of an asset and has all your framework requires to discover a report and its worker on the Web. At any rate, a flat out URL contains the plan and all necessary components of the scheme_specific_part of the URL. It might likewise contain any of the discretionary bits of the scheme_specific_part.

With a relative URL, you give a shortened archive address that, when naturally joined with a "base location" by the framework, turns into a total location for the record. Inside the relative URL, any part of the URL might be precluded. The program consequently fills in the missing bits of the overall URL utilizing comparing components of a base URL. This base URL is normally the URL of the report containing the relative URL, yet might be another archive indicated with the base tag.

11.1 Relative document directories

Another basic type of an overall URL precludes the main slice and at least one registry names from the start of the record pathname. The catalog of the base URL is naturally accepted to supplant these missing segments. It's the most well-known condensing, on the grounds that most creators place their assortment of archives and subdirectories of help assets in a similar catalog way as the landing page. For instance, you may have an exceptional/subdirectory containing FTP records referred to in your report.

Regular "speck slice" pathname documentations additionally let you express the current index ("./") and catalog over the current registry (parent; "../") in a relative URL. The current index documentation is seldom utilized, since it is repetitive. Be that as it may, the parent documentation allows you to set the objective URL to catalogs in different parts of the file system chain of command.

11.2 Using relative URLs

Relative URLs are something beyond a composing accommodation. Since they are comparative with the current worker and registry, you can move the whole arrangement of reports to another index or much another worker and never need to change a solitary relative connection. Envision the troubles on the off chance that you needed to go into each source report and change the URL for each connection each time you move it. We'd detest utilizing hyperlinks! Utilize relative URLs at every possible opportunity.

Chapter 12. Creating Hyperlinks

Utilize the HTML/XHTML (a) tag to make connects to different reports and to name secures for section identifiers inside records.

12.1 The (a) Tag of Hyperlinks

You will utilize the (a) label most regularly with its href characteristic to make a hypertext connection, or hyperlink, for short, to somewhere else in a similar report or to another record. In these cases, the current report is the wellspring of the connection; the estimation of the href trait, a URL, is the objective.

You may stumble into the expressions "head" and "tail," which reference the objective and wellspring of a hyperlink. This naming plan accepts that the referred to archive (the head) has numerous tails that are implanted in many referring to reports all through the Web. We track down this naming show confounding and adhere to the idea of source and target records all through this book.

The alternate way you can utilize the (a) tag is with the name trait to stamp a hyperlink target, or piece identifier, in an archive. This technique, albeit part of the HTML 4 and XHTML guidelines, is gradually surrendering to the id quality which allows you to check almost any component, including passages, divisions, structures, etc., as a hyperlink target.

The principles let you utilize both the name and href credits inside a solitary (a) tag, characterizing connect to another record and a section identifier inside the current archive. We advise against this, since it over-burdens a solitary tag with numerous capacities, and a few programs will be unable to deal with it.

All things being equal, utilize two (a) labels when such a need emerges. Your source will be clearer and adjust and will work better across a more extensive scope of programs.

12.2 Allowed content of (a) tag

Between the (a) tag and its necessary end tag, you may put just customary content, line breaks, pictures, and headings. The program delivers these components ordinarily, yet with the expansion of some enhancements to demonstrate that it is a hyperlink to another archive. For example, the well-known graphical programs regularly underline and shading the content and draw a hued line around pictures that are encased by (a) labels.

While the permitted substance may appear to be confined (the powerlessness to put style markup inside (a) tag is somewhat grave, for example), most programs let you put pretty much anything inside (a) label that bodes well. To be agreeable with the HTML 4 and XHTML guidelines, place the (a) tag inside other markup labels, not the inverse.

For instance, while most programs figure out one or the other minor departure from this anchor subject:

12.3 The href attribute of (a) tag

Utilize the href property to indicate the URL of the objective of a hyperlink. It worth is any legitimate archive URL, outright or relative, including a part identifier or a JavaScript code section. In the event that the client chooses the substance of the (a) tag, the program will endeavor to recover and show the report demonstrated by the URL determined by the href ascribe or execute the rundown of JavaScript articulations, techniques, and capacities.

12.4 The name and id attributes of (a) tag

Utilize the name and id ascribes with the (a) tag to make a part identifier inside a report. When made, the section identifier turns into a likely objective of a connection.

Preceding HTML 4.0, the best way to make a part identifier was to utilize the name quality with the (a) tag. With the appearance of the id trait in HTML 4.0, and its capacity to be utilized with practically any tag, any HTML or XHTML component can be a section identifier. The (a) tag holds the name quality for noteworthy purposes and praises the id quality also. These ascribes can be utilized conversely, with id being the more "current" form of the name characteristic. Both name and id can be indicated related to the href characteristic, permitting a solitary (a) to be both a hyperlink and a section identifier.

A simple method to think about a section identifier is as the HTML simple of the go to proclamation name regular in many programming dialects. The name quality inside the (a) tag or the id trait inside the (a) or different labels puts a name inside a report. At the point when that mark is utilized in connect to that archive, it is what might be compared to advising the program to go to that name.

The estimation of the id or name characteristic is any character string, encased in quotes. The string should be a novel mark, not reused in some other name or id quality in a similar archive, despite the fact that it tends to be reused in various records.

Notice we set the anchor in a part header of a probably enormous record. It's a training we urge you to use for all significant areas of your work for simpler reference and future brilliant preparing, like computerized extraction of points.

In fact, you don't need to put any archive content inside the (a) tag with the name characteristic, since it essentially denotes an area in the report. Practically speaking, a few programs overlook the label except if some archive content - a word or expression, even a picture - is between the (a) and (/a) labels. Thus, it's most likely a decent thought to have at any rate one displayable component in the body of any (a) tag.

12.5 The event attributes of (a) tag

There are various occasion overseers incorporated into the cutting edge programs. These overseers watch for specific conditions and client activities, for example, a tick of the mouse or when a picture completes the process of stacking into the program window. With customer side JavaScript, you may incorporate chosen occasion overseers as qualities of specific labels and execute at least one JavaScript orders and capacities when the occasion happens.

With the anchor (a) tag, you may relate JavaScript code with various mouse- and console related occasions. The estimation of the occasion controller is - encased in quotes - one or an arrangement of semicolon-isolated JavaScript articulations, strategies, and capacity references that the program executes when the occasion happens.

A mainstream, but basic, utilization of the on Mouse Over occasion with a hyperlink is to print an extended portrayal of the label's objective in the JavaScript-mindful program's status box. Ordinarily, the program shows the often secretive objective URL there at whatever point the client disregards the mouse pointer (a) label's substance:

We contend that the substance of the actual label ought to clarify the connection, however there are times when window space is tight and an extended clarification is useful, for example, when the connection is in a list of chapters.

12.6 The rel and rev attributes of (a) tag

The rel and fire up ascribes express a conventional relationship and bearing among source and target reports. The rel property determines the relationship from the source archive to the objective, and the fire up characteristic indicates the relationship from the objective to the source. The two credits can be set in a solitary (a) tag, and the program may utilize them to exceptionally modify the presence of the anchor content or to consequently build record route menus. Different apparatuses likewise may utilize these ascribes to fabricate uncommon connection assortments, tables of substance, and lists.

The estimation of either the rel or fire up characteristic is a space-isolated rundown of connections. The genuine relationship names and their implications are up to you: they are not officially tended to by the HTML or XHTML guidelines. For instance, a report that is important for an arrangement of records may incorporate its relationship.

The relationship from the source to the objective is that of moving to the following report; the opposite relationship is that of moving to the past record.

These archive connections are likewise utilized in the connection tag in the record (head). The connection tag sets up the relationship without really making connect to the objective report; the (a) tag makes the connection and permeates it with the relationship credits.

Scarcely any programs exploit these ascribes to adjust the connection appearance. Nonetheless, these credits are an incredible method to record joins you make, and we prescribe that you set aside the effort to embed them at whatever point conceivable.

12.7 The target attribute of (a) tag

The objective trait allows you to determine where to show the substance of a chose hyperlink. Usually utilized related to outlines or various program windows, the estimation of this trait is the name of the edge or window wherein the referred to record ought to be stacked. In the event that the named casing or window exists, the record is stacked in that casing or window. If not, another window is made, given the predefined name, and the report is stacked in that new window. For more data, including a rundown of unique objective names.

12.8 The title attribute of (a) tag

The title characteristic allows you to determine a title for the archive to which you are connecting. The estimation of the trait is any string, encased in quotes. The program may utilize it while showing the connection, maybe blazing the title when the mouse ignores the connection. The program may likewise utilize the title quality while adding this connect to a client's hotlist.

The title quality is particularly helpful for referring to a usually unlabeled asset, for example, a picture or a non-HTML report. For instance, the program may remember the accompanying title for this usually silent picture show page:

In a perfect world, the worth indicated should coordinate with the title of the referred to report, yet it's not needed.

12.9 The charset, hreflang, and type attributes of (a) tag

As indicated by the HTML 4 and XHTML guidelines, the charset characteristic determines the character encoding utilized in the report that is the objective of the connection. The estimation of this quality should be the name of a standard character set.

The hreflang quality might be determined just when the href property is utilized. Like the lang trait, its worth is an ISO standard two-character language code. Dissimilar to the lang property, the hreflang characteristic doesn't address the language utilized by the substance of the tag. All things being equal, it indicates the language utilized in the record referred to by the href quality.

The sort quality indicates the substance kind of the asset referred to by the (a) tag. It is worth is any MIME encoding type. For instance, you may illuminate the program that you are connecting to a plain ASCII report with.

The program may utilize this data while showing the referred to archive, or may even present the connection distinctively dependent on the substance type.

12.10 The coords and shape attributes of (a) tag

These are two additional credits characterized in the HTML and XHTML norms for the (a) label that are not upheld by the current, mainstream programs. Like the credits of similar names for territory tag, arrange and shape ascribes characterize an area of impact for the (a) tag. These credits should just be utilized with the (a) label when that tag is essential for the substance of a guide tag, as depicted later in this section.

Generally, clients of graphical programs choose and execute a hyperlink by pointing and tapping the mouse gadget on the area of the program show characterized by the anchor. What is less notable is that you may pick a hyperlink, among different items in the program window, by squeezing the Tab key and afterward actuate that interface by squeezing the Return or Enter key. With the tab file trait, you may reorder the succession where the program ventures through to each protest when the client presses the Tab key. The estimation of this characteristic is a number more prominent than nothing. The program begins with the article whose tab record is 1 and travels through different items in expanding request.

With the entrance key trait, you may choose an option "hot-key" that, when squeezed, actuates the particular connection. The estimation of this quality is a solitary character that is squeezed related to an "alt" or "meta" key, contingent upon the program and figuring stage. In a perfect world, this character ought to show up in the substance of the (a) tag; provided that this is true, the program may decide to show the character contrastingly to demonstrate that it is a hot-key.

You make a hyperlink to another record with the (a) tag and its href quality, which characterizes the URL of the objective report. The substance of the (a) tag are introduced to the client in some particular way to demonstrate that the connection is accessible.

While making connect to another archive, you ought to consider adding the title, rel, and fire up qualities to the (a) tag. They help report the connection you are making and permit the program to adorn the presentation anchor substance.

13.1 Linking Within a Document

Making a connection inside a similar report or to a particular section of another record is a two-venture measure. The initial step is to make the objective part; the second is to make connect to the piece.

13.2 Creating Effective Links

A record becomes hypertext by throwing in a couple of connections similarly that water becomes soup when you toss in a couple of vegetables. In fact, you've met the objective, however the result may not be entirely tasteful.

Embedding secures into your records is something of a craftsmanship, requiring great composing abilities, HTML/XHTML ability, and a structural feeling of your archives and their connections to others on the Web. Viable connections stream flawlessly into a report, discreetly providing extra perusing freedoms to the user without upsetting the current archive. Inadequately planned connections shout out, interfere with the progression of the source archive, and by and large disturb the user.

While there are as many connecting styles as there are creators, here are a couple of the more famous approaches to interface your archives. All complete two things: they give the user speedy admittance to related data, and they tell the user how the connection is identified with the current substance.

13.3 Lists of Links

Maybe the most widely recognized approach to introduce hyperlinks is in arranged or unordered records in the style of a list of chapters or rundown of assets.

Two schools of style exist. One places the whole rundown thing into the source anchor; the other shortens the thing and places a shorthand expression in the source anchor. In the previous, ensure you keep the anchor content straightforward; in the last mentioned, utilize an immediate composing style that makes it simple to insert the connection.

In the event that your rundown of connections turns out to be excessively long, consider arranging it into a few sub records gathered by theme. Per users would then be able to examine the themes (set off, maybe, as (h3) headers) for the fitting rundown and afterward check that rundown for the ideal archive.

The elective rundown style is significantly more graphic, yet additionally more tedious, so you must be cautious that it doesn't wind up jumbled. It once in a while gets hard to peruse a source HTML record, and it will turn out to be considerably more drawn-out with XHTML.

Envision the messiness in the event that we'd utilized anchors with piece identifiers for every one of the subtopics in the rundown thing clarifications. In any case, everything looks flawless and effectively safe when shown by the program, for example, with Internet Explorer.

This more enlightening way of introducing a connection list makes a decent attempt to bring per users into the connected archive by giving a more full taste of what they can hope to discover. Since each rundown component is longer and requires more filtering by the user, you should utilize this style sparingly and significantly limit the quantity of connections.

Utilize the concise rundown style while introducing enormous quantities of connections to a very much educated crowd. The second, clearer style is more qualified to fewer connections for which your readership is less knowledgeable in the current subject.

In the event that you're not gathering joins into records, you're most likely sprinkling them all through your report. Alleged inline joins are more with regards to the genuine soul of hypertext, since they empower per users to check their present spot in the report, visit the connected theme in more profundity or track down a superior clarification, and afterward return to the first and keep perusing. That is exceptionally customized data handling.

The greatest error made by fledgling creators, be that as it may, is to over-burden their records with connections and treat them as though they are emergency signals requesting to be squeezed. You may have seen this way of connecting; HTML pages with "here" everywhere, similar to the frenzy ridden.

As connections, phrases like "click here" and "likewise accessible" are sans content and irritating. They make the individual who is checking the page for a significant connection read all the encompassing content to really discover the reference.

The better, more refined style for an inline connect is to make each one contain a thing or thing/action word state identifying with the current point. Look at how kumquat cultivating and industry news references are dealt with.

A brisk sweep quickly yields valuable connects to industry's previous ten years. There is no compelling reason to peruse the encompassing content to comprehend where the connection will take you. For sure, the promptly encompassing substance in our model, concerning most inline joins, serves just as syntactic sugar on the side of the installed joins.

Installing joins into the overall talk of an archive requires more exertion to make than interface records. You must really comprehend the substance of the current just as the objective archives, have the option to communicate that relationship in only a couple words, and afterward wisely fuse that interface at some critical spot in the source record. Ideally this key spot is the place where you may expect the client is prepared to intrude on their perusing and pose an inquiry or solicitation more data. To make matters considerably more troublesome, especially for the conventional tech essayist, this type of writer per user discussion is best when introduced in dynamic voice (he, she, or it plans something for an article versus the item having something done to it). The exertion used is beneficial, however, bringing about more enlightening, effectively read reports. Keep in mind, you'll compose the record once, however it will be understood thousands, if not millions, of times.

It has gotten popular to utilize pictures and symbols rather than words for interface substance. For example, rather than "next," you may utilize a symbol of a little pointing hand. A connect to the landing page isn't finished without an image of a little house. Connections to looking through instruments should now contain an image of an amplifying glass, question mark, or optics. And each one of those blazing, GIF-vivified little notices!

Oppose falling prey to the "Mount Everest condition" of embedding pictures just in light of the fact that you can. Once more, it's a matter of setting. In the event that you or your archive's users can't tell initially what relationship a connection has with the current report, you've fizzled. Utilize adorable pictures for joins sparingly, reliably, and just in manners that help per users filter your archive for significant data and leads. Likewise be ever careful that your pages might be perused by somebody from almost any place on Earth (maybe past, even) and that pictures don't interpret reliably across social limits. (At any point hear what the "alright" hand sign normal in the United States intends to a Japanese individual?)

Making steady iconography for an assortment of pages is an overwhelming errand, one that definitely should be finished with the help of somebody officially educated in visual plan. Trust us, the sort of brain that produces clever code and composes XHTML well is once in a while fit to making excellent, convincing symbolism. Track down a decent visual architect; your pages and per users will profit immensely.

Regularly, a picture set inside an anchor basically turns out to be essential for the anchor content. The program may modify the picture in some unique manner (generally with an extraordinary line) to alarm the user that it is a hyperlink, yet clients click the picture similarly they click a text based hyperlink.

The HTML and XHTML guidelines give an element that allows you to install various connections inside a similar picture. Clicking various regions of the picture makes the program connect to various objective records. Such mouse-touchy pictures, known as picture maps, open up an assortment of innovative connecting styles.

There are two different ways to make picture maps, known as worker side and customer side picture maps. The previous, empowered by the ismap quality for the picture tag, expects admittance to a worker and related picture map preparing applications. The last is made with the usemap characteristic for the picture tag, alongside comparing guide and zone labels. Since interpretation of the mouse position in the picture to a connect to another record occurs on the client's machine, customer side picture maps don't need an uncommon worker association and can even be executed in non-web conditions, for example, on a neighborhood hard drive.

16.1 Server-Side Image Maps

You add a picture to an anchor just by setting a picture tag inside the body of the (a) tag. Make that inserted picture into a mouse-touchy one by adding the ismap characteristic to the picture tag. This exceptional picture trait tells the program that the picture is a unique guide containing more than one connection. (The ismap characteristic is disregarded by the program if the picture tag isn't inside (a) tag.)

At the point when the client clicks some spot inside the picture, the program passes the directions of the mouse pointer alongside the URL determined in the (a) tag to the record worker. The worker utilizes the mouse pointer directions to figure out which record to convey back to the program.

When ismap is utilized, the href trait of the containing (a) label should contain the URL of a worker application or, for some HTTP workers, a connected guide document that contains arrange and connecting data. On the off chance that the URL is just that of a regular archive, mistakes may result and the ideal report will doubtlessly not be recovered.

The directions of the mouse position are screen pixels checked from the upper-left corner of the picture starting with (0, 0). The directions are added to the furthest limit of the URL, gone before by a question mark.

16.2 Server-side considerations

With mouse-touchy ismap-empowered picture maps, the program is needed to pass along just the URL and mouse directions to the worker. Changing over these directions into a particular record is taken care of by the archive worker.

The transformation cycle varies among workers and isn't characterized by the HTML or XHTML guidelines.

You need to talk with your web worker overseers and maybe even read your worker's documentation to decide how to make and program a picture map. Most workers accompany some product utility, normally situated in a cgi-container/imagemap registry, to deal with picture maps. What's more, the majority of these utilization a book document containing the picture map districts and related hyperlinks that is referred to by your picture map URL to deal with the picture map inquiry.

Every touchy district of the picture map is portrayed by a mathematical shape and characterizing arranges in pixels, like the circle with its middle point and range, the square shape's upper-left and lower-right edge organizes, and the loci of a polygon. All directions are comparative with the upper-left corner of the picture (0, 0). Each shape has a connected URL.

A picture map handling application regularly tests each shape as per the pattern in which it shows up in the picture record and returns the report determined by the relating URL to the program if the client's mouse x, y arranges fall inside the limits of that shape. That implies it's OK to cover shapes; simply know which takes priority. Likewise, the whole picture need not be covered with delicate districts: if the passed facilitates don't fall inside a predefined shape, the default archive gets sent back to the program.

This is only one model for how a picture guide might be prepared and the adornment records needed for that cycle. Kindly group with your website admin and worker manuals to find how to execute a worker side picture map for your own reports and framework.

The conspicuous drawback to worker side picture maps is that they require a worker. That implies you need admittance to the necessary HTTP worker or its/cgi-container/catalog, which isn't generally accessible. Also, worker side picture maps limit movability, since not all picture map handling applications are something very similar.

Worker side picture maps likewise mean deferrals for the client while perusing, since the program should stand out enough to be noticed to deal with the picture facilitates. That is regardless of whether there's no move to make, for example, a segment of the picture that isn't hyperlinked and doesn't lead anyplace.

Customer side picture maps experience the ill effects of none of these challenges. Empowered by the usemap quality for the picture tag, and characterized by unique guide and zone augmentation labels, customer side picture maps let creators remember for their archives a guide of directions and connections that depict the delicate areas of a picture. The program on the customer PC interprets the directions of the mouse position inside the picture into an activity, like stacking and showing another archive. Furthermore, extraordinary JavaScript-empowered ascribes give an abundance of enhancements for customer side picture maps.

To make a customer side picture map, incorporate the usemap characteristic as a feature of the picture tag. It is worth is the URL of a guide fragment in a HTML report that contains the guide arranges and related connection URLs. The report in the URL recognizes the HTML archive containing the guide; the part identifier in the URL distinguishes the guide to be utilized. Regularly, the guide is in a similar archive as the actual picture, and the URL can be decreased to the section identifier: a pound sign (#) trailed by the guide name.

16.4 The (map) Tag of mouse-sensitive images

For customer side picture guides to work, you should remember some place for your report a bunch of directions and URLs that characterize the mouse-delicate locales of a customer side picture map and the hyperlink to take for every area that is clicked by the client. Incorporate those directions and connections as estimations of characteristics in traditional (a) labels or exceptional zone labels; the assortment of area details or (a) labels are encased inside the guide tag and its end tag (/map). The (map) fragment may show up anyplace in the body of the record.

All the more explicitly, the guide tag may contain either an arrangement of zone labels or customary HTML/XHTML content including (a) labels. You can't blend and match territory labels with ordinary substance. Traditional substance inside the guide tag might be shown by the program; region labels won't. In the event that you are worried about similarity with more seasoned programs, utilize just guide labels containing territory labels.

In the event that you do put a labels inside a guide tag, they should incorporate the shape and coords ascribes that characterize a district inside the articles that reference the map tag.

16.5 The name attribute of the map tag

The estimation of the name quality in the map tag is the name utilized by the usemap trait in a picture or article tag to find the picture map particular. The name should be remarkable and not utilized by another guide in the record, yet more than one picture guide may reference a similar guide particulars.

16.6 The area Tag of mouse-sensitive images

The guts of a customer side picture map are the area labels inside the guide fragment. These territory labels characterize each mouse-delicate area and the move the program should make in the event that it is chosen by the client in a related customer side picture map.

The district characterized by a territory label acts actually like whatever other hyperlink: when the client moves the mouse pointer over the area of the picture, the pointer symbol will change and the program may show the URL of the connected hyperlink in the status box at the lower part of the program window. Regions of the customer side picture map not characterized in at any rate one area tag are not mouse-delicate.

16.7 The alt attribute of the area tag

Like its cousin for the picture tag, the alt trait for the area label lets appends a book name to the picture, besides for this situation the name is related with a specific territory of the picture. The well-known programs show this mark to the client when the mouse disregards the region, and it might likewise be utilized by a nongraphic program to introduce the customer side picture map as a rundown of connections recognized by the alt lab.

16.8 The coords attribute of the area tag

The required coords property of the area tag characterizes directions of a mouse-touchy district in a customer side picture map. The quantity of directions and their importance rely on the district's shape as controlled by the shape quality, examined later in this section. You may characterize hyperlink locales as square shapes, circles, and polygons inside a customer side picture map. The suitable qualities for each shape are recorded.

As an option in contrast to the mouse, a client may pick a record "area of interest, for example, a hyperlink inserted in a picture map, by squeezing the Tab key. When picked, the client initiates the hyperlink by squeezing the Return or Enter key. Of course, the program steps to every area of interest according to the pattern in which where they show up in the record.

Initially presented by Internet Explorer with the taborder trait, and now normalized as the tabindex attribute, you may change that default request. The estimation of the property is a whole number showing the situation of this region in the general tab grouping for the report.

Upheld by Internet Explorer just and not piece of either the HTML 4 or XHTML guidelines, notab regions get disregarded as the client presses the Tab key to move the cursor around the archive. Something else, this region will be essential for the selecting arrangement. The characteristic is valuable, obviously, in mix with the nohref property.

The notab and taborder ascribes were upheld by Internet Explorer variant 4. The program's variant 5 backings tabindex also.

Utilize the shape quality to characterize the state of a picture guide's mouse-touchy district: a circle (circ or circle), polygon (poly or polygon), or square shape (rect or square shape).

The estimation of the shape quality influences how the program deciphers the estimation of the coords characteristic. On the off chance that you do exclude a shape characteristic, the worth default is expected. As indicated by the norm, default implies that the region covers the whole picture. Practically speaking, the programs default to a rectangular territory and hope to discover four coords values. What's more, on the off chance that you don't indicate a shape and do exclude four directions with the tag, the program overlooks the region through and through.

Truth be told, Netscape is the solitary program that even perceives the shape esteem default to give a catch-all zone to clicks that fall outside the wide range of various characterized areas of interest. Since regions are in a "first-come, first-served" request in the guide tag, you should put the default region last. Else, it conceals all zones that continue in your picture map.

The programs are remiss in their execution of the shape names. Netscape 4, for instance, doesn't perceive "square shape" however perceives "rect" for a rectangular shape. Consequently, we suggest that you utilize the condensed names.

Not at all like its worker side ismap partner, shouldn't the customer side picture map tag (img usemap) be remembered for (a) tag. In any case, it could be, so you can smoothly deal with programs that can't cycle customer side picture maps.

For instance, Mosaic or early forms of Netscape basically load a record named main.html if the client taps the map.gif picture referred to in the accompanying source section. The all-inclusive programs, then again, will partition the picture into mouse-touchy locales, as characterized in the related guide and connection to a specific name anchor inside the equivalent main.html archive if the picture map district is chosen by the client.

To make a picture map in reverse viable with all picture map-competent programs, you may likewise incorporate customer side and worker side handling for a similar picture map. Fit programs will respect the quicker customer side preparing; any remaining programs will disregard the usemap characteristic in the img tag and depend upon the referred to worker interaction to deal with client determinations in the customary manner.

Chapter 18. Effective Use of Mouse-Sensitive Images

Probably the most outwardly convincing pages on the Web have mouse-delicate pictures: maps with area that when clicked, for instance, lead to more data about a country or town or result in more insight concerning the area and who to contact at a local office of a business. We've seen a mouse-delicate picture of a style model whose different dress parts lead to their particular index passages, complete with itemized portrayal and sticker price for requesting.

The visual idea of mouse-delicate pictures combined with the requirement for a compelling interface implies you ought to emphatically consider having a craftsman, a UI architect, and surprisingly a human-factors master assess your mouse-touchy symbolism. At any rate, participate in a touch of client testing to ensure individuals realize where to snap to move to the ideal report. Ensure the "mouse capable" regions of the picture show this to the client utilizing a reliable visual component. Think about utilizing borders, drop shadows, or shading changes to demonstrate those zones that can be chosen by the client.

At long last, consistently recollect that the choice to utilize mouse-delicate pictures is an express choice to bar text-based and picture limited programs from your pages. This incorporates programs interfacing with the Internet by means of moderate modem associations. For these individuals, downloading your excellent pictures is just excessively costly. To hold back from disappointing a developing populace, ensure any page that has a mouse-touchy picture has a book just identical effectively open from a connection on the picture empowered form. Some insightful website admins even give separate pages for clients leaning toward full designs versus generally text.

Another extensible type of a HTML connect that doesn't utilize the (a) tag is one that makes the worker scan a data set for a report that contains a client indicated catchphrase or words. A HTML report that contains such a connection is known as an accessible record.

19.1 The isindex Tag (Deprecated)

Not, at this point upheld in the HTML 4 or XHTML norms, creators all at once utilized the isindex tag to pass watchwords alongside an internet searcher's URL to the worker. The worker at that point coordinated with the catchphrases against an information base of terms to choose the following archive for show. The present creators generally use structures to pass data to the worker and supporting projects.

The client types a rundown of room isolated watchwords into the field gave. At the point when the client presses the Enter key, the program consequently attaches the question rundown to the furthest limit of a URL and passes the data to the worker for additional handling.

While the HTML and XHTML guidelines just permit the censured isindex tag to be put in the archive header, most programs let the tag show up anyplace in the report and addition the hunt field in the substance stream where the isindex tag shows up. This advantageous expansion allows you to add guidelines and other helpful components prior to giving the client the genuine pursuit field.

The program gives a main brief simply above or to one side of the client passage field. Web Explorer's default brief, for instance, is "You can look through this file. Type the keyword(s) you need to look for".

That default brief isn't the awesome all events, so it is feasible to transform it with the brief characteristic.

When added to the isindex tag, the estimation of the brief property is the line of text that goes before the catchphrase section field set in the record by the program.

More established programs will disregard the brief property, however there is little motivation not to incorporate a superior brief string for your more state-of-the-art readership.

Not very many archives remain solitary. All things considered, an archive is generally essential for an assortment of records, each associated by one or a few of the hypertext strands we depict in this section. One record might be a piece of a few assortments, connecting to certain reports and being connected to by others. Per users move between the report families as they follow the connections that interest them.

You set up an unequivocal connection between two records when you interface them. Scrupulous creators utilize the rel quality of the (a) tag to demonstrate the idea of the connection. Moreover, two different labels might be utilized inside a record to additionally explain the area and relationship of an archive inside a report family. These labels, base and connection, are put inside the body of the head tag.

20.1 The base Header Element

As we recently clarified, URLs inside a report can be either total (with each component of the URL expressly given by the creator) or relative (with specific components of the URL excluded and provided by the program). Ordinarily, the program fills in the spaces of an overall URL by drawing the missing pieces from the URL of the current record. You can change that with the base tag.

The base tag ought to show up just in the report header, not its body substance. The program from that point utilizes the predefined base URL, not the current record's URL, to determine every single relative Url, remembering those found for (a), (img), (connection), and (structure) labels. It likewise characterizes the URL that will be utilized to determine inquiries in accessible archives containing the isindex tag.

20.2 Using base in Relationships

The main justification utilizing base is to guarantee that any overall URLs inside the record will resolve into a right archive address, regardless of whether the actual report is moved or renamed. This is especially significant while making an archive assortment. By setting the right base tag in each report, you can move the whole assortment among indexes and even workers without breaking the entirety of the connections inside the records.

You additionally need to utilize the base tag for an accessible archive (isindex) on the off chance that you need client questions presented to a URL unique in relation to the host report.

An archive that contains both the isindex tag and other relative URLs may have issues if the overall URLs are not comparative with the ideal record preparing URL. Since this is generally the situation, don't utilize relative URLs in accessible records that utilization the base tag to determine the inquiry URL for the report.

Making data more open is the absolute most significant nature of HTML and its descendants XHTML. The dialects' great assortment of text style and designing apparatuses assist you with getting sorted out your data into records per users rapidly get, output, and concentrate, potentially with robotized program specialists.

Past adorning your content with specific content labels, HTML and XHTML additionally give a rich arrangement of devices that assist you with getting sorted out content into designed records. There's not much or strange about records. Indeed, the excellence of records is their effortlessness. They're founded on regular rundown ideal models we experience each day, for example, an unordered clothing list, requested guidance records, and word reference like definition records. All are natural, agreeable methods of getting sorted out content. All give amazing intends to rapidly getting, examining, and separating relevant data from your web records.

21.1 Unordered Lists

Like a clothing or shopping list, an unordered rundown is an assortment of related things that have no extraordinary request or grouping. The most well-known unordered rundown you'll discover on the Web is an assortment of hyperlinks to different archives. Some normal point, as "Related Kumquat Lovers' Sites," partners the things in an unordered rundown, yet they have no organization among themselves.

21.2 The (ul) Tag

The (ul) label signs to the program that the accompanying substance, finishing with the (/ul) tag, is an unordered rundown of things. Inside, everything in the unordered rundown is distinguished by a main (li) tag. Something else, almost anything HTML/XHTML-wise goes, including different records, text, and media components.

Commonly, the program adds a main projectile character and organizations everything on another line, indented fairly from the left edge of the archive. The genuine delivering of unordered records, albeit comparable for the mainstream programs isn't directed by the principles, so you shouldn't get mad attempting to achieve precise situating of the components.

Precarious HTML creators some of the time utilize settled unordered records, with and without (li)-labeled things, to exploit the programmed, progressive indenting. You can deliver some genuinely smooth content fragments that way. Simply don't rely upon it for all programs, including future ones. Or maybe, it's ideal to utilize the boundary property with a style definition in the passage (p) or division (div) tag to indent non rundown segments of your record.

21.3 Ordered Lists

Utilize an arranged rundown when the succession of the rundown things is significant. A rundown of guidelines is a genuine model, as are tables of substance and arrangements of report references or endnotes.

21.4 The (ol) Tag

The run of the mill program arranges the substance of an arranged rundown actually like an unordered rundown, then again, actually the things are numbered rather than bulleted. The numbering begins at one and is increased by one for each progressive arranged rundown component labeled with (li).

HTML 3.2 presented various highlights that give a wide assortment of requested records. You can change the beginning estimation of the rundown and select any of five distinctive numbering styles.

It ought to be very clear to you at this point that the (li) tag characterizes a thing in a rundown. It's the all-inclusive tag for list things in arranged (ol) and unordered (ul) records, as we talked about before, and for catalogs (dir) and menus (menu), which we examine in detail later in this part.

Since the finish of a rundown component can generally be construed by the encompassing archive structure, most creators discard the closure (/li) labels for their rundown components. That bodes well since it gets simpler to add, erase, and move components around inside a rundown. Notwithstanding, XHTML requires the end tag, so it's ideal to become acclimated to remembering it for your records.

Albeit all inclusive in importance, there are a few contrasts and limitations to the utilization of the (li) tag for each rundown type. In unordered and requested records, what follows the (li) tag might be almost anything, including different records and numerous passages. Commonly, on the off chance that it handles space by any means, the program progressively indents settled rundown things, what's more, the substance in those things is advocated to the deepest indented edge.

Catalog and menu records are another matter. They are arrangements of short things like a solitary word or straightforward content snippet and that's it. Subsequently, (li) things inside (dir) and (menu) labels may not contain different records or other square components, including passages, preformatted squares, or structures.

Clean reports, completely consistent with the HTML and XHTML principles, ought not to contain any content or other record thing inside the unordered, requested, registry, or menu records that isn't contained inside an (li) tag. Most programs are open minded toward infringement to this standard, yet then you can't consider the program liable for consistent delivering for excellent cases, by the same token.

Similarly as you can change the slug or numbering style for the entirety of the things in an unordered or requested show, you likewise can change the style for singular things inside those rundowns. With requested records, you additionally can change the estimation of the thing number. As you'll see, the blends of changing style and numbering can prompt an assortment of helpful rundown structures, especially when included with settled records. Do note, nonetheless, that the guidelines have censured these ascribes in regard to their CSS partners.

Besides inside registries or menus, records settled inside different records are fine. Menu and index records can be implanted inside different records.

Indents for each settled rundown are combined, so take care not to settle records excessively; the rundown substance could rapidly transform into a slender strip of text flush against the correct edge of the program report window.

23.1 Nested Unordered List

The things in each settled unordered rundown might be gone before by an alternate projectile character at the carefulness of the program. For instance, Internet Explorer Version 2 for Macintosh utilized an exchanging arrangement of empty, strong roundabout, and square shots for the different homes in the accompanying source section (other programs to date haven't been as innovative)

You can change the projectile style for each unordered rundown and in any event, for singular rundown things (see the sort quality conversation prior in this section), however the collection of slugs is restricted. For instance, Internet Explorer for Windows utilizes a strong plate paying little heed to the settling level.

Of course, programs number the things in arranged records starting with the Arabic numeral 1, settled or not. It would be incredible if the principles numbered settled arranged records in some objective, sequential way. For instance, the things in the second home of the third primary arranged rundown may be progressively numbered.

With the kind and worth credits, notwithstanding, you do have much more scope by the way you make settled arranged records. A fantastic model is the conventional style for illustrating, which utilizes the wide range of methods of numbering things offered by the sort property.

Chapter 24. Definition Lists

HTML and XHTML likewise support a rundown style altogether not the same as the arranged and unordered records we've talked about up until now: definition records. Like the sections you find in a word reference or reference book, total with text, pictures, and other interactive media components, the definition list is the ideal method to introduce a glossary, rundown of terms, or other name/esteem records.

24.1 Appropriate List Usage

All in all, utilization unordered records for:

• Hotlists and other connection assortments

• Short, non-sequenced gatherings of text

• Emphasizing the high places of an introduction

As a rule, utilize requested records for:

• Tables of substance

• Instruction successions

• Sets of successive segments of text

• Assigning numbers to short expressions that can be referred to somewhere else

By and large, use definition records for:

• Glossaries

• Custom slugs (make the thing after the (dt) label a symbol estimated projectile picture)

• Any rundown of name/esteem sets.

Templates are the manner in which distributing experts deal with the generally speaking "look" of their distributions - foundations, text styles, colors, etc. - from a solitary page to colossal assortments of reports. Most work area distributing programming support templates, as do the mainstream word processors. All work area distributers and visual creators deserving at least moderate respect are out there making website pages. So the cry-to-arms was inescapable: "Which mean HTML has no templates?!"

From its sources, HTML zeroed in on content over style. Creators are urged to stress over giving top notch data and leave it to the program to stress over introduction. We unequivocally ask you, as well - as we do all through this book - to receive that way of thinking in your reports, particularly those bound for the World Wide Web. Try not to confuse style with substance.

Notwithstanding, while utilization of the textual style tag and related credits like shading produce intense introduction impacts, templates, when prudently applied, carry consistency and request to entire report assortments, just as to singular records. Keep in mind that introduction is to support user. Indeed, even the first architects of HTML comprehended the interchange among style and meaningfulness. For example, per users can rapidly recognize area heads in a report when they are encased in header labels like h2, which the cutting edge programs present in enormous and frequently intense sort. Templates broaden that introduction with a few extra impacts, counting tones, a more extensive determination of textual styles, even sounds so clients can stunningly better recognize components of your archive. Yet, above all, templates let you control the introduction ascribes for every one of the labels in a report - for a solitary archive or an entire assortment of numerous records, and from a solitary expert.

In mid-1996, the World Wide Web Consortium set up a draft proposition characterizing Cascading Style Sheets (CSS) for HTML. This draft proposition immediately developed into a suggested standard, which the business program makers rushed to misuse. In mid-1998, the W3C stretched out the first determination to make CSS2 which incorporates introduction norms for an assortment of media other than the natural onscreen program, alongside a few different improvements.

Up to now, nonetheless, no program or web specialist completely follows the CSS2 standard. Since we understand that inevitable consistence with the W3C standard is likely, we'll cover every one of the parts of the norm in this section, regardless of whether they are not yet upheld by any program. As usual, we'll mean obviously what is genuine, what is proposed, and what is really upheld.

What we can't do is disclose to you everything the CSS2 standard gives. Like JavaScript, the Cascading Style Sheet standard merits its very own Definitive Guide. Or maybe, we center here on the components of templates that sway HTML and XHTML all in all and the well-known GUI-based programs, Internet Explorer and Netscape Navigator, specifically. These include most of the CSS2 standard. What's left out are conversations of other media. We reveal to you how to tailor your archives to other media, yet we don't go into the points of interest, for example, the CSS2 properties that control paging gadgets like printers or aural templates that oversee the introduction of substance through discourse combination. Try not to misunderstand us; these are intriguing and significant points. They simply go past our contract.

25.1 The Elements of Styles

At the least complex level, a style is simply a standard that advises the program how to deliver a specific label's substance. Each tag has various style properties related with it, whose qualities characterize how that tag is delivered by the program. A standard characterizes a particular incentive for at least one properties of a tag. For instance, most labels have a shading property, the estimation of which characterizes the shading Netscape or Internet Explorer may use to show the substance of the tag. Different properties incorporate textual styles, line separating, edges, borders, sound volume, and voice, which we depict in detail later in this part.

We expressly kept away from the expression "show" here on the grounds that it indicates visual introduction, though the CSS2 standard endeavors to recommend various methods of introducing the labeled substance of a record.

There are three different ways to connect a style to a tag: inline styles, record level styles, and outer templates. You may utilize at least one templates for your archives. The program either combines the style definitions from each style or rethinks the style trademark for a label's substance. Styles from these different sources are applied to your report, consolidating and characterizing style properties that course from outer templates through neighborhood archive styles, finishing with inline styles. This course of properties and style rules brings about the standard's name: Cascading Style Sheets.

We cover the syntactic rudiments of the three template procedures here. We dig all the more profoundly into the suitable utilization of inline, report level, and outside templates toward the finish of this part.

25.2 Inline Styles: The style Attribute

The inline style is the most straightforward approach to append a style to a tag - simply incorporate a style property with the tag alongside a rundown of properties and their qualities. The program utilizes those style properties and qualities to deliver the substance of simply this occurrence of the tag.

This sort of style definition is classified "inline" on the grounds that it happens with the tag as it shows up in the report. The extent of the style covers the substance of that label as it were. Since inline styles are sprinkled all through your archive, they can be hard to keep up. Utilize the style quality sparingly and just in those uncommon conditions when you can't accomplish similar impacts in any case.

25.3 Document-Level Style Sheets

The genuine force of templates turns out to be more apparent when you place a rundown of introduction rules inside the top of a record. Encased inside their own (style) and (/style) end labels, purported "record level" templates influence overall the very labels inside that archive, with the exception of labels that contain an abrogating inline style characteristic. XHTML-based report level templates get uniquely encased in CDATA areas of your archives.

The style label should show up inside the (head) of a report. Everything between the style and (/style) labels is viewed as a component of the style rules to be applied to the archive. To be totally right, the substance of the style tag are not HTML or XHTML and are not limited by the ordinary principles for markup content. The style tag, essentially, allows you to embed unfamiliar substance into your archive that the program uses to organize your labels.

25.4 External Style Sheets

You may likewise put style definitions, similar to our archive level template model for the (h1) labels, into a book record with the MIME kind of text/css and import this "outside" template into your reports. Since an outer template is a different document and is stacked by the program over the organization, you can store it anyplace, reuse it frequently, and even utilize others' templates. Yet, generally significant, outside templates enable you to impact the presentation styles not just of all connected labels in a solitary report, however for a whole assortment of archives.

For all of the reports in our assortments, we can advise the program to peruse the substance of the gen_styles.css record, which thus will shading all the (h1) label substance blue and render the content in italic. Obviously, that will be genuine just if the client's machine is equipped for these style stunts, they are utilizing a styles-cognizant program like Netscape or Internet Explorer, and the style isn't abrogated by a report level or inline style definition.

You can stack outside templates into your record in two distinct manners: connected or imported.

25.5 Media-Specific Styles

Other than the media characteristic for the style tag, the CSS2 standard has two different highlights that let you apply distinctive templates relying upon the specialist or gadget that will deliver your report. Along these lines, for example, you can have one style or entire template produce results when your report gets delivered on a PC screen, and another arrangement of styles for when the substance get punched out on a braille printer. Furthermore, what might be said about those cells on the Web?

Like the media property for the style label that influences the whole template, you can determine whether the client's report processor will load and utilize an imported template.

"Client specialist." Web records get delivered on a wide range of gadgets nowadays, including the well-known program, braille printers, TVs, and projectors, to give some examples.

Do that by adding a media-type watchword or a progression of comma-isolated catchphrases to the furthest limit of the @import at-rule. For example, the accompanying model lets the client specialist choose to import and utilize the discourse combination template or a typical PC show and print template in the event that it can deliver the predefined media types.

25.6 Linked Versus Imported Style Sheets

From the start, it might create the impression that connected and imported templates are same, utilizing distinctive punctuation for a similar usefulness. This is valid in the event that you utilize only one connection tag in your record. Notwithstanding, exceptional CSS2-standard principles become an integral factor on the off chance that you incorporate at least two connection labels inside a solitary record, despite the fact that the current programs don't keep the principles yet.

With one connection tag, the program should stack the styles in the referred to template and organization the record appropriately, with any archive level and inline styles abrogating the outside definitions. With at least two connection labels, the program should give the client a rundown of all the (interface) ed templates. The client at that point chooses one of the connected sheets, which the program loads and uses to organize the record; the other (interface) ed templates get disregarded.

Then again, the styles-cognizant program converges, rather than isolating, numerous @imported templates to frame a solitary arrangement of style rules for your archive. The last imported template outweighs everything else if there are copy definitions among the templates. Consequently, if the outer gen_styles.css template determination advises the program to make (h1) substance blue and italic, and spec_styles.css advises the program to make (h1) text red, at that point the (h1) label substance will seem red and italic. Furthermore, on the off chance that we later characterize another tone, say yellow, for (h1) labels in a report level style definition, the (h1) labels will all be yellow, and italic. Falling impacts.

By and by, the well-known programs treat connected templates actually like imported ones by falling their belongings. The programs don't right now allow you to browse among connected decisions. Imported styles supersede connected outside styles, similarly as the record level and inline styles abrogate outer style definitions.

Web Explorer 4 and Netscape Navigator 4 and past help the (link) tag to apply an outer template to a report. Neither Netscape Navigator nor Internet Explorer support various (connect) ed templates as proposed by the CSS2 standard. All things considered, they course all the (connect) ed templates, with rules in later sheets superseding rules in prior sheets.

Netscape Navigator overlooks all at-rules and their substance, including @import and @media, yet measures other style decides that you may incorporate previously or after the at-rule inside the style tag. Web Explorer praises the @import just as the @media at-rules, for both record level and outside sheets, permitting sheets to be settled.

Accomplishing media-explicit styles through outside templates with current Netscape programs is sad. Expect, in this way, that the vast majority who have Netscape will deliver your reports on a typical PC screen, so make that medium the default one. At that point insert any remaining media-explicit styles, like those for print or braille, inside @media at-rules, so Internet Explorer and other CSS-agreeable specialists will appropriately choose styles dependent on the delivering medium. The lone other option is to make media-explicit (style) labels inside each record.

Flee, don't walk, away from that thought. We simply trust the CSS2 standard will win soon so that templates, previously bewildering to most, will get at any rate that amount less confounding.

25.8 Style Comments

Remarks are welcome inside the style tag and in outside templates, however don't utilize standard HTML remarks; templates aren't HTML. Or maybe, encase style remarks starting with the arrangement/* and finishing with */, as we did in past model. (Those of you who know about the C programming language will perceive these remark markings.) Use this remark grammar for both archive level and outer templates. Remarks may not be settled.

We suggest recording your styles at whatever point conceivable, particularly in outer templates. At whatever point the chance exists that your styles might be utilized by different creators, remarks make it a lot more obvious your styles.

25.9 Handling Style-less Browsers

In our archive level style models, you presumably saw that we set the style definition inside a remark tag (! - - and -). That is on the grounds that albeit the more seasoned, style-less programs will disregard the style label itself, they will show the style definitions. Obviously, your reports won't go over well when the principal half of the show contains all your style rules.

The more current, styles-cognizant programs overlook HTML remarks inside a style tag. Style-less programs might be with us for quite a while to come, so it's presumably best to put your report level style rules inside remarks. HTML remarks ought not to be utilized in outer templates.

For XHTML, record level styles should be encased in a CDATA segment rather than in HTML remarks.

You may import more than one outside template and join them with archive level and inline style impacts from multiple points of view. Their belongings course (thus, the name, obviously). You may indicate the text style type for our model (h1) tag, for example, in an outside style definition, though its tone may come from a record level template.

Template impacts are not aggregate, nonetheless: of the numerous styles which may characterize various qualities for a similar property - colors for the substance of our model tag, for example - the one that outweighs everything else can be found by keeping these principles.

The connection between style properties and customary label ascribes is practically difficult to foresee. Template directed foundation and closer view tones - regardless of whether characterized remotely, at the record level, or inline - abrogate the different shading ascribes that may show up inside a tag. However, the adjust quality of an inline picture for the most part outweighs a style-directed arrangement.

There is a staggering bunch of style and label introduction quality blends. You need a precious stone ball to foresee which mix wins and which loses the priority fight. The guidelines of excess and style versus trait priority are not plainly clarified in the W3C CSS2 standard, nor is there a reasonable example of priority carried out in the styles-cognizant programs. This is especially disastrous since there will be an all-encompassing period, maybe quite a while, in which clients might utilize a styles-cognizant program. Creators should carry out the two styles and non-style introduction controls to accomplish similar impacts.

In any case, our proposal is to run - as quick as possible - away from one-shot, inline, confined sorts of introduction impacts like those managed by the (font) tag and shading trait. They have filled their brief need; it's currently an ideal opportunity to bring consistency (without the agony!) back into your report introduction. Use styles. It's the HTML way.

A style rule is comprised of at any rate three essential parts: a selector, which is the name of the markup component that the style rule influences, trailed by a wavy support ({}) encased, semicolon-isolated rundown of at least one style property:value sets. For example, we may characterize the tone for the substance of all the level-1 header components of our report. In this model, h1 is the selector which is likewise the name of the level-1 header component, shading is the style property, and green is the worth. Slick and clean. Attempt it. It truly works!

Properties need at any rate one worth, yet may incorporate at least two qualities. Separate numerous qualities with a space, as is accomplished for the three qualities that characterize property2 in our first model. A few properties necessitate that different qualities be isolated with commas.

Current styles-cognizant programs disregard letter case in any component of a style rule. Thus, H1 and h1 are a similar balloter, and COLOR, shading, ColOR, and cOLor are identical properties. At one time, convention dictated that HTML writers compose selector names in capitalized characters, like H1, P, and STRONG. This show is as yet normal and is utilized in the W3C's own CSS2 archive.

Current norms direct, in any case, especially for XML-agreeable records, that component names be promoted precisely as characterized by their separate DTDs. With XHTML, for example, all component names (h1, p, or solid, for example) are lowercase, so their separate CSS2 selectors should be in lowercase. We'll submit to these last shows.

Any substantial component name (a label name short its encasing (and) characters and properties) can be a selector. You may incorporate more than one label name in the rundown of selectors, as we clarify in the accompanying segments.

26.1 Contextual Selectors

Typically, the styles-cognizant program applies record level or imported styles to a label's substance any place they show up in your report, regardless of setting. Notwithstanding, the CSS2 standard characterizes an approach to have a style applied just when a tag happens inside a specific setting inside a record, for example, when it is settled inside different labels.

To make a context oriented selector, list the labels in the request where they ought to be settled in your archive, peripheral label first. At the point when that settling request is experienced by the program, the style properties will be applied to the last tag in the rundown.

For instance, here's the manner by which you may utilize logical styles to characterize the exemplary numbering arrangement utilized for traces: capitalized Roman numerals for the external level, capital letters for the following level, Arabic numerals for the following, and lower-case letters for the deepest level:

There are basic connections in your archives you can't expressly tag. The drop-cap is a typical print style, however how would you choose the main letter in a section? There are ways, yet you need to recognize every single occasion independently. There is no tag for the main line in a section. What's more, there are events where you may need the program to consequently produce content, for example, to add the prefix "Thing #" and naturally number everything in an arranged rundown.

CSS2 presents four new pseudo-components that let you characterize exceptional connections and styles for their presentation: first-line, first-letter, previously, then after the fact. Pronounce each as a colon-isolated postfix of a standard markup component.

In a specialized paper you should characterize one section style for the theoretical, another for conditions, and a third for focused citations. None of the section labels may have an unequivocal setting in the record so you could recognize it from the others. Or maybe, you may characterize each as an alternate style class.

Notice first in the model that characterizing a class is just an issue of annexing a period-isolated class name as an addition to the label name as the selector in a style rule. Not at all like the XHTML-agreeable selector, which the name of the standard tag and should be in lowercase, the class name can be any grouping of letters, numbers, and hyphens, however, should start with a letter. Careful, however, case matters, so that theoretical isn't equivalent to AbsTRact. Furthermore, classes, similar to selectors, might be incorporated with different selectors, isolated by commas, as in the third model.

The solitary limitation on classes is that they can't be settled: p.equation.centered isn't permitted, for instance. Due to its help of JavaScript templates, Netscape can't deal with class names that end up coordinating JavaScript catchphrases. The class "dynamic," for example, produces a blunder in Netscape.

Appropriately, the principal rule in the model makes a class of section styles named "dynamic" whose text will be italic and indented from the left and right edges by a half-centimeter. Essentially, the subsequent section style class "condition" educates the program to focus the content and to utilize the

Symbol typeface to show the content. The last style rule makes a style with focused content and half-centimeter edges, applying this style to all level one headers just as making a class of the (p) label named focused with that style.

Practically all HTML labels acknowledge the id characteristic, which allots an identifier to the component that is one of a kind inside the report. This identifier can be the objective of a URL, utilized via robotized report preparing apparatuses and can likewise be utilized to determine a style rule for the component.

Inside your report, you could utilize (h1 id=blue) to make a blue heading, or add (id=yellow) to practically any tag to turn it yellow. You can blend and match both class and id credits, giving you a restricted capacity to apply two autonomous style rules to a solitary component.

At the point when HTML was initially imagined, nobody knew it would be so effective or be approached to deal with such countless sorts of archives, programs, and media. While it has facial hair up outstandingly under the requests of web clients, HTML 4.0 has extended the extent that it can to oblige new innovation. While HTML 4.0 is dwindling, XHTML 1.0 stands prepared to step in, intended to deal with nearly anything web creators can cook up.

While HTML is a static markup language with a fixed arrangement of labels, XHTML is only one bunch of labels characterized with XML, the Extensible Markup Language. Utilizing XML, you can characterize labels to address practically any sort of information or report, not exactly what the HTML fashioners had as a main priority when they created HTML. Need to catch melodic documentation? Synthetic formulae? Coordinated circuits? XML can deal with this and let you coordinate your new markup labels with XHTML, making crossover archives that will in any case work with existing programs. By adding XSL (Extensible Style Sheets), you can even show programs how to show all your new labels.

MICROSOFT

ACCESS

A BEGINNERS GUIDE TO MICROSOFT ACCESS STEP-BY-STEP

BY John Davis

Introduction

Microsoft Access is a database software that is used to save records for reporting, referencing and analysis MS access stores data in specific format, database specific to Access based Access Jet Database. With Microsoft Access, you can analyze big amount of data faster and more efficiently than with Excel or different forms of spreadsheets.

If you've been considering a database software to your enterprise, otherwise you're locating that traditional spreadsheets just aren't slicing it anymore, Microsoft Access simply what you're seeking out. Let's have a brief look of fundamental functions of access and how its functions can help the businesses to be more productive.

Access is maximum popular for its tables, forms and queries. The database tables are similar to spreadsheets, so that you shouldn't have an awful lot hassle the usage of the simple features of the program. But, it does take time to examine and master the full features. Tables have two things rows and columns. Rows represents set of related data and each row has the same structure in the whole table and every column in the table has the data value of particular type they both bifurcate categories, groups and more. Whilst putting in place a database, you may list the difficulty count of every column, just as you'll with a spreadsheet, and add as many columns as you'd like. While this is completed, every row leaves room for more statistics enter. One characteristic that users surely like is they don't want to finalize the tables manually. Additionally, get right of entry to has a query feature that permits facts to be mixed from more than one desk, and you could even specify the conditions. This saves numerous time due to the fact you don't ought to glance through rows and rows of statistics.

If you're already the usage of a spreadsheet application like Excel, you're acquainted with the benefits of organizing your facts. However, allows appearance further into some of the particular obligations that you can perform with Access.

- Preserve all records for each patron or purchaser, which include addresses, invoices, payment and order statistics.
- Keep track of economic statistics without having a separate software program application. If you have the overall Microsoft workplace Suite, you may even set fee reminders.
- Manage advertising and income thanks to having all customer facts within the database. Ship out flyers, emails and coupons and song how customers respond.
- Track manufacturing and inventory with the aid of getting into statistics on shipments and additionally knowing whilst it's time to order more of a specific product.

Run reviews and analyses using the reports and charts. You can basically run a document on something within a rely of mins, such as customers who are behind on price.

Access follows most, however not all, conventional database terminology. The terms database, table, file, field, and value imply a hierarchy from largest to smallest. These identical terms are used with simply all database structures. Generally, the phrase database is a computer term for a set of statistics concerning a sure subject matter or business software. Databases assist you prepare this associated records in a logical style for clean get entry to and retrieval. Databases aren't only for computer systems. There are also manual databases; we once in a while discuss with those as guide filing structures or manual database systems. These submitting systems usually consist of people, papers, folders, and submitting shelves paper is the important thing to a manual records base machine. In manual database systems, you commonly have inside and outside baskets and some sort of formal filing method. You get entry to statistics manually by means of opening a report cabinet, taking away a document folder, and locating the proper piece of paper. Users fill out paper forms for input, perhaps via using a keyboard to input records that's printed on forms. You discover information via manually sorting the papers or by way of copying statistics from many papers to some other piece of paper (or even into an Excel spreadsheet). You can use a spreadsheet or calculator to investigate the data or show it in new and thrilling approaches. An get entry to database is not anything greater than an automated model of the filing and retrieval capabilities of a paper submitting gadget. Get right of entry to databases store facts in a carefully defined shape. Access tables store a diffusion of various sorts of information, from easy lines of text (which includes call and cope with) to complex statistics (together with photographs, sounds, or video snap shots). Storing records in a unique layout allows a database management gadget (DBMS) like access to show statistics into beneficial statistics. Tables function the number one statistics repository in an get admission to database. Queries, bureaucracy, and reports offer get right of entry to the records, enabling a person to feature or extract records and supplying the statistics in beneficial methods. Most developers upload macros or visible primary for programs (VBA) code to paperwork and reviews to make their get right of entry to applications simpler to apply. A relational database control machine (RDBMS), such as get entry to, stores statistics in related tables. As an example, a table containing worker data (names and addresses) can be related to a desk containing payroll facts (pay date, pay amount, and check range). Queries allow the consumer to invite complicated questions From these related tables, with the answers displayed as onscreen forms and printed reports. One of the essential differences between a relational database and manual filing system device is that, in a relational database machine, data for single individual or item may be saved in separate tables. As an example, in affected person control system, the affected person's name, deal with, and other contact statistics is possibly to be stored in extraordinary table from the table protecting affected person treatments. In fact, the table holds all treatment information for all patients, and a patient identifier (typically more than a few) is used to appearance up an individual affected person's treatments in the treatment table. In Microsoft Access, a database is the general box for the data and related gadgets. It's greater than the gathering of tables, however a database consists of many sorts of objects, including queries, forms, reviews, macros, and code modules. As you open an MS Access database, the objects (tables, queries, indexes, procedures, triggers and so on) inside the database are provided that allows you to work with. You may open several copies MS Access to on the identical time and simultaneously work with a couple of database, if its needed.

Chapter 1

1.1 Database Development

Microsoft Access follows most, however now not all, conventional database terminology. The terms database, table, record, field, and value imply a hierarchy from largest to smallest. These identical terms are used with simply all database structures.

1.1.1 Tables

A table is only a box for raw information (known as data), just like a folder in a person manual submitting filing system. Every table in ma Microsoft Access database incorporates information approximately a single topic, which include employees or merchandise, and the statistics within the table is organized into rows and columns. In Access, a table is an entity. As you layout and build access databases, or even when running with an updated existing Microsoft software application, you must think of how the tables and different database items represent the physical entities controlled via your database and the way the entities relate to one another. When you create a table, you can view the table in a spreadsheet like shape, referred to as a datasheet, comprising rows and columns. Even though a datasheet and a spreadsheet are superficially similar, a datasheet is a completely one of a kind of item.

1.1.2 Records and fields

A datasheet is split into rows (known as records) and columns (called fields), with the first row (the heading on top of each column) containing the names of the fields in the database. Each row is a single document containing fields which might be associated with that document. In a manual gadget, the rows are individual forms (sheets of paper), and the fields are equivalent to the blank areas on a printed shape which you fill in.

Each column is a field that consists of many properties that explain the type of data contained within the field and how access need to handle the field's information. Those properties encompass the name of the (Agency) and the type of information inside the field (textual content). A field may additionally consist of different properties as well. As an instance, the location fields property tells to Access the maximum number of characters a location field can hold.

1.1.3 Values

At the intersection of a record and a field is a value the real information detail. As an example, if you have a field known as Agency, an employer name entered into that field might constitute one facts value. Positive guidelines govern how statistics is contained in an get entry to table.

1.2 Relational Database

Microsoft Access is a relational database management system. Access data is stored in related tables, wherein facts in one table (including clients) is related to facts in every other table (such as Orders). Access continues the relationships among associated tables, making it clean to extract a consumer and all of the client's orders, without losing any facts or pulling order records not owned via the Client. Multiple tables simplify data entry and reporting by way of lowering the enter of redundant data. Via defining two tables for a software that uses purchaser records, for instance, you don't need to store the clients call and deal with every time the purchaser purchases an item.

When you've created the tables, they need to be associated with each other. As an example, if You have a client's table and a sales table, you can relate the two tables the usage of a common discipline between them. In this case, customer number might be an amazing discipline to have in each tables. This will let you see income in the sales table where the client number suits the clients table.

The benefit of this model is which you don't ought to repeat key attributes about a client's (like patron call, cope with, metropolis, nation, zip) on every occasion you add a new file to the income desk. All you need is the client number. Whilst a client changes address, for instance, the deal with modifications simplest in one record within the clients table.

Keeping apart information into more than one tables within a database makes a system less complicated to hold due to the fact all statistics of a given type are in the equal table. By using taking the time to properly segment data into a couple of tables, you revel in an enormous reduction in design and work time. This procedure is known as normalization.

Chapter 2

2.1 Microsoft Database Objects

In case you're new to databases (or maybe in case you're an experienced database user), you need to understand some key concepts earlier than starting to construct Microsoft Access databases. The access records- base consists of six sorts of pinnacle-degree items, which encompass the facts and gear which you want to use access:

- Table: Holds the actual records
- Query: Searches for, sorts, and retrieves unique records
- Form: lets you input and display facts in a custom designed layout
- Report: shows and prints formatted data
- Macro: Automates obligations without programming
- Module: carries programming statements written within the VBA programming language

2.1.1 Tables

As you've located in advance on previous chapter, tables function the primary facts repository in an get admission to database. You have interaction with tables through a unique type of object known as a statistics- sheet. Even though not a permanent database object, a datasheet displays a table's content material in a row and column layout, just like an Excel worksheet. A datasheet displays a desk's records in a raw shape, without alterations or filtering. The Datasheet view is the default mode for displaying all fields for all records. You can scroll via the datasheet using the directional keys on your keyboard. You can also display associated facts in other tables even as in a datasheet. In addition, you could make modifications to the displayed statistics.

2.1.2 Queries

Queries extract facts from a database. A question selects and defines a collection of information that satisfy a sure circumstance. Most forms and reviews are primarily based on queries that integrate, filter, or type information earlier than it's displayed. Queries are often known as from macros or VBA procedures to trade, add, or delete database facts. An example of a query is while a person at the sales workplace tells the database, "show me all clients, in alphabetical order through name, who are placed in Massachusetts and acquired a few issue over the last six months" or "show me all customers who sold Chevrolet vehicle fashions within the past six months and show them looked after by using purchaser name after which by sale date." In place of asking the query in plain English, someone makes use of the question by means of instance (QBE) approach. While you enter commands into the query fashion designer window and run the question, the question interprets the commands into established query Language (SQL) and retrieves the favored information.

2.2 Information access and show forms

Data entry forms help customers get facts into a database table quick, easily, and accurately. Facts-access and show paperwork offer a greater based view of the records than what a datasheet offers. From this dependent view, database data may be considered, added, modified, or deleted. Entering information via the records-access paperwork is the maximum common manner to get the information into the database table. Facts access forms may be used to limit get admission to sure fields within the desk. Paperwork can also be better with records validation guidelines or VBA code to test the validity of your facts before it's delivered to the database table. Most users opt to enter records into facts-entry bureaucracy instead of into Datasheet perspectives of tables. Paperwork frequently resemble acquainted paper documents and can useful resource the person with statistics-entry responsibilities. Bureaucracy make records entry easy to recognize by means of guiding the consumer via the fields of the desk being up to date. Examine simplest forms are frequently used for inquiry purposes. These paperwork display positive fields inside a table. Showing some fields and not others way that you could restrict a consumer's get entry to touchy statistics while permitting get right of entry to different fields within the same table.

2.3 Reports

Reports provides you facts in PDF-fashion formatting. Get right of entry to permits for a super amount of pliability while creating reports. As an instance, you can configure a document to list all records in a given table (consisting of a client's table), or you may have the file include simplest the data assembly sure criteria (together with all clients residing in Arizona). You try this by way of basing the document on a query that selects handiest the facts wished via the file. Reviews frequently integrate more than one tables to provide complicated relationships among unique sets of records. An example is printing a bill. The clients table provides the customer's call and address (and different applicable records) and associated statistics within the sales table to print the man or woman line-object facts for every product ordered. The record also calculates the sales totals and prints them in a particular format. Moreover, you may have got entry to output records into an invoice file, a broadcast record that summarizes the invoice.

2.4 Macros and VBA

Just as Excel has macros and VBA programming functionality, Microsoft get admission to has its equivalents. That is where the genuine energy and versatility of Microsoft get admission to statistics analysis resides. Whether or not you're the use of them in custom capabilities, batch evaluation, or automation, macros and VBA modules can add a customized flexibility that is hard to fit the usage of every other method. As an instance, you could use macros and VBA to routinely perform redundant analyses and habitual analytical approaches, leaving you free to work on other tasks. Macros and VBA also can help you reduce the risk of human mistakes and to make certain that analyses are preformed the same way every time. Starting in bankruptcy 22, you will discover the advantages of macros and VBA, and learn how you could use them to schedule and run batch analysis.

2.5 Planning for database objects

To create database gadgets, which include tables, forms, and reviews, you first complete a sequence of layout obligations. The better your design is, the higher your utility could be. The extra you watched through your design, the quicker and greater correctly you may whole any system. The layout method isn't a few important evil, neither is its rationale to provide voluminous amounts of documentation. The sole intent of designing an object is to supply a clear path to comply with as you enforce it.

Chapter 3

3.1 Five Step Design Model

The 5 design steps defined in this segment offer a strong basis for developing database applications together with tables, queries, forms, reports, macros, and easy VBA modules.

The time you spend on each step depends absolutely on the situations of the database you're building. As an instance, occasionally customers provide you with an example of a file they need printed from Microsoft Access database, and the assets of information at the report are so obvious that designing the document takes a few minutes. Other instances, especially when the users' requirements are complicated or the enterprise strategies supported by the software require an exceptional deal of research, you could spend many days on Step 1.

Step 1: the general design—from concept to reality

All software developers face similar problems, the primary of that is figuring out a way to meet the desires of the end consumer. It's important to apprehend the general user requirements earlier than zeroing in on the details.

For example, your users can also ask for a database that supports the following obligations:

- Coming into and retaining clients information facts (name, address, and economic history)
- Entering and retaining income data (income date, payment approach, total quantity, patron identification, and other fields)
- Coming into and retaining sales line item records (information of objects bought)
- Viewing facts from all of the tables (income, clients, sales line objects, and bills)
- Asking all types of questions about the records in the database
- Generating a month-to-month invoice record
- Producing a consumer income history
- Generating mailing labels and mail-merge reviews

When reviewing these eight duties, you can need to remember different peripheral responsibilities that weren't referred to with the aid of the person. Earlier than you soar into designing, sit down and find out how the present process works. To perform this, you have to do a thorough wishes analysis of the existing gadget and how you would possibly automate it. Prepare a sequence of questions that deliver perception to the patron's commercial enterprise and the way the customer uses his facts. For instance, whilst considering automating any type of commercial enterprise, you might ask those questions:

- What reviews and paperwork are presently used?
- How are sales, customers, and other data presently stored?
- How are billings processed?

As you ask these questions and others, the patron will probably bear in mind different things about the commercial enterprise which you must understand. A walkthrough of the present procedure is likewise helpful to get a sense for the commercial enterprise. You may have to pass back numerous times to take a look at the present procedure and the way the personnel work. As you put together to finish the remaining steps, hold the patron worried permit the users know what you're doing and ask for enter on what to perform, ensuring it's in the scope of the person's needs.

Step 2: record design

Even though it can appear odd to start with reviews, in lots of instances, users are extra inquisitive about the printed output from a database than they're in every other aspect of the utility. Reports often consist of each bit of data managed via a utility. Due to the fact reports have a tendency to be complete, they're often the fine way to acquire vital statistics approximately a database's necessities. Whilst you see the reviews that you'll create on this section, you may surprise, "Which comes first, the bird or the egg?" Does the document layout come first, or do you first decide the statistics gadgets and text that make up the file? Without a doubt, those gadgets are considered at the equal time. It isn't critical the way you lay out the records in a document. The extra time you're taking now, how- ever, the less complicated it will likely be to assemble the file. A few people pass so far as to place grid- lines on the record to discover precisely where they want every little bit of records to be.

Step 3: statistics design

The subsequent step within the layout phase is to take a stock of all the facts needed through the reviews. One of the great techniques is to listing the information gadgets in each file. As you accomplish that, take cautious word of gadgets which might be protected in multiple report. Make certain which you preserve the identical name for a data item this is in more than one document because the facts object is truly the equal item.

As you can see by comparing the form of consumer records wanted for every document, there are many common fields. Maximum of the patron records fields are located in each reports. Table 1.1 indicates only some of the fields that are utilized in every report those related to customer information. Due to the fact the related row and field names are the identical, you could easily ensure which you have all the statistics objects. Although finding items without problems isn't critical. For this small database, it will become very important when you have to address large tables containing many fields.

Table # 3.1: Clients related data items found in reports

Clients Report	Invoice Report
Clients Name	Clients Name
Street	Street
City	City
State	State
Zip Code	Zip Code
Phone Number	Phone Numbers
Email Address	
Web Address	
Last Sales Date	
Sales Tax Rate	

As you could see when you observe the sort of income statistics wished for the file, some items (fields) are repeating (for example, the Product bought, quantity bought, and charge of object fields). Every bill could have more than one objects, and every of these objects desires the identical kind of records—number ordered and rate according to object. Many sales have multiple bought object. Also, every bill may additionally include partial payments, and it's viable that this charge information can have a couple of lines of charge statistics, so these repeating objects may be put into their own grouping.

Table # 3.2: Dales data found in reports

Invoice report	Item data
Invoice date	Product purchased
Sales date	Quantity purchased
Invoice date	Description of item
Payment method	Item price
Salesperson	Discount per item
Discounts	
Tax location	
Product purchased	
Quantity purchased	
Description of item	
Price of item	
Payment type	
Payment date	
Payment amount	
Expiration date	

You may take all the individual items which you discovered within the income records institution inside the preceding section and extract them to their very own institution for the bill report. Desk 1.2 indicates the statistics related to every line object. After extracting the client facts, you could flow on to the sales records. In this case, you need to research handiest the invoice document for information items which are precise to the sales. Table 1.2 lists the fields inside the record that include information approximately income.

Step 4: desk design

Now for the hard part: you ought to decide which fields are needed for the tables that make up the reports. While you examine the multitude of fields and calculations that make up the various files you have, you begin to see which fields belong to the various tables inside the database. (You already did tons of the preliminary paintings by means of arranging the fields into logical corporations.) For now, encompass each field you extracted. You'll want to add others later (for numerous motives), although positive fields won't appear in any table. It's essential to understand that you don't want to feature each little bit of data into the database's tables. As an instance, users may additionally need to feature excursion and different out of office days to the database to make it smooth to recognize which employees are available on a selected day. But, it's very smooth to burden an application's initial layout by means of incorporating too many ideas at some stage in the initial development levels. Because get entry to tables are so smooth to modify later, it's in all likelihood high quality to place aside noncritical items until the preliminary design is entire. Generally speaking, it's not difficult to deal with consumer requests after the database improvement project is underway.

When you've used each record to display all the records, it's time to consolidate the data through purpose (for instance, grouped into logical organizations) after which evaluate the facts throughout those functions. To do that step, first examine the client data and combine all its different fields to create a single set of information objects. Then do the identical component for the sales information and the line-object statistics.

Table # 3.3: Comparing data items

Clients data	Invoice data	Line items	Payment info
Client agency name	Invoice number	Product purchased	Payment
Street	Date of sale	Quantity purchased	Date of payment
City	Date of invoice	Description of purchasing	Amount of purchaser
State	Discount	Price of item	Credit card no.
Zip code	Tax rate	Each item discount	Date of expiry
Phone no.			
Email address			
Web address			
Discount rate			
Client since			
Sales tax			

Consolidating and comparing records is a superb manner to begin developing the character desk, but you've got a lot more to do. As you learn greater about the way to carry out a records design, you furthermore might study that the clients data ought to be break up into two organizations. Some of these gadgets are used best once for every customer, even as other items may additionally have more than one entries. An example is the income column the charge statistics could have multiple traces of statistics. You need to in addition ruin these forms of records into their own columns, accordingly, separating all associated types of items into their personal columns an instance of the normalization part of the design process. For example, one customer may have multiple contacts with the agency or make a couple of payments in the direction of a single sale. Of course, we've already damaged the records into 3 classes: patron statistics, invoice statistics, and line object information.

Remember the fact that one patron can also have a couple of invoices, and every bill might also have multiple line gadgets on it. The bill data class consists of data about man or woman income and the road-objects category incorporates data about each invoice. Word that those 3 columns are all related; as an example, one customer can have more than one invoices, and each invoice may also require multiple line items.

The relationships among tables can be different. For instance, each income bill has one and simplest one customer, whilst each purchaser can also have a couple of income. A comparable courting exists among the sales bill and the line items of the invoice.

Database table relationships require a unique field in each tables worried in a dating. A unique identifier in every table allows the database engine to properly join and extract associated facts. Best the income desk has a completely unique identifier (bill wide variety), which means that that you need to add at the least one field to every of the other tables to serve as the link to other tables for example, adding a client identification area to the clients desk, including the same subject to the invoice table, and establishing a relationship among the tables through purchaser id in each desk. The database engine makes use of the connection between customers and invoices to attach customers with their invoices. Relationships among tables are facilitated through the usage of key fields.

Table # 1.4: table with keys

Clients data	Invoice data	Line items	Payment Data
Client ID	Invoice ID	Invoice ID	Invoice ID
Clients Name	Clients ID	Line No	Payment type
City	Date of invoice	Description of purchasing	Amount of purchaser
State	Discount	Price of item	Credit card no.
Zip code	Tax rate	Each item discount	Date of expiry
Phone no.			
Email address			
Web address			
Discount rate			
Client since			
Sales tax			

With an know how of the need for linking one fields to another table, you could upload the desired key fields to every group. Table 1.4 shows two new agencies and hyperlink fields created for each organization of fields. Those linking fields, known as primary keys and foreign keys, are used to hyperlink these tables together.

The sector that uniquely identifies each row in a desk is the number one key. The corresponding subject in a related desk is the foreign key. In our instance, customer identification inside the clients table is a number one key, even as customer identification within the Invoices desk is a foreign key. Let's count on a certain record within the clients table has 12 in its purchaser id discipline. Any document inside the Invoices desk with 12 as its purchaser identification is "owned" by client 12. With the key fields brought to each desk, you could now find a discipline in every table that hyperlinks

204

It to other tables within the database. For instance, desk 1.4 indicates patron identity in both the clients desk (where it's the number one key) and the invoice desk (in which it's a foreign key). You've diagnosed the 3 middle tables on your device, as reflected with the aid of the first three columns in table 1.4. That is the general, or first, cut in the direction of the very last desk designs. You've also created an additional truth desk to maintain the sales payment statistics. Commonly, charge details aren't part of an income bill. Taking time to properly layout your database and the tables contained within it is arguably the maximum essential step in developing a database orientated application. By using designing your database efficaciously, you preserve manage of the records, disposing of highly priced records entry mistakes and proscribing your records entry to essential fields.

Although this e book isn't geared toward coaching database principle and all its nuances, this is a great region to briefly describe the artwork of database normalization. You'll study the info of normalization in chapter four, however in the interim you must recognize that normalization is the method of breaking records down into constituent tables. Earlier on this chapter you read approximately how many access builders upload distinctive information, which includes customers, invoice statistics, and invoice line objects, into one big table. A massive table containing varied statistics quickly will become unwieldy and difficult to keep updated. Because a patron's telephone variety seems in every row containing that customer's facts, more than one updates need to be made when the phone variety modifications.

Step 5: form layout

Once you've created the data and set up table relationships, it's time to design your paperwork. Paperwork are made up of the fields that can be entered or considered in Edit mode. Generally speaking, your get entry to displays must appearance a lot like the paperwork utilized in a manual device.

Whilst you're designing bureaucracy, you need to area three types of objects onscreen:

- Labels and textual content box information access fields: The fields on get entry to forms and reports are called controls.
- Unique controls (command buttons, more than one-line text boxes, alternative buttons, list containers, take a look at packing containers, commercial enterprise graphs, and images).
- Graphical gadgets to decorate the forms (colorations, lines, rectangles, and 3 dimensional results).

Preferably, if the form is being evolved from a present revealed shape, the get right of entry to information-access form have to resemble the broadcast form. The fields ought to be in the identical relative area at the screen as they may be inside the published counterpart. Labels show messages, titles, or captions. Text boxes provide an area in which you may kind or show textual content or numbers that are contained in your database. Test boxes suggest a situation and are either unchecked or checked. Different kinds of controls available with access consist of command buttons, list packing containers, combo packing containers, choice buttons, toggle buttons, and choice agencies.

Chapter 4

4.1 Microsoft Access Tables

4.2 Table types

To Microsoft Access, a table is constantly just a table. But to your Microsoft Access application, specific tables serve special functions. A database table fits into one among 3 sorts: an item table, a transaction table, or a join desk. Knowing what form of table, you're developing facilitates to decide the way you create it.

4.2.1 Object tables

Object tables are the most not unusual. Each record of this type of desk holds facts that relates to real world object. A client is a real-world object, and a record in a table named tblclient holds information approximately of the client. The fields in an object table mirror the traits of the item they represents. A city field in the table describes one function of the client particularly, the actual city where the purchaser is. Whilst developing an object table, reflect on consideration on the traits of that item that make it precise or that are vital.

4.2.2 Transaction tables

The next most common type of table is a transaction table. Each file of a transaction table holds information about an event. Like you have placed the order for a book so placing an order for a book is an instance of an event. To hold the info of all the orders, you may have a table named tblbookorders. Transaction tables almost constantly have a date/time discipline due to the fact while the event happened is usually a crucial piece of records to file. Some other not unusual form of subject is an area that refers to an objects table, together with a connection with the purchaser in tblclient that placed the order. While growing a transaction table, consider the statistics created via the occasion and who changed into involved.

4.2.3 Join tables

Join tables are the easiest to design and are vitally critical to a highly designed database. Normally bearing on tables is a simple procedure: a client orders a book, for instance, and you could without problems relate that order to that client. However now and again the connection isn't so clear. A book might also have many authors, and an author may additionally have many books. Whilst this relationship exists, called a many-to-many relationship, a be a part of table sits in the center of the two tables. A be part of desk typically has a call that displays the association, including tblauthorbook. A be part of desk normally has only 3 fields: a completely unique subject to become aware of every file, a reference to 1 side of the association, and a connection with the other side of an affiliation.

4.3 Creating a new table

Developing database tables is as much art as it's far science. Obtaining a very good working know how of the clients necessities is a fundamental step for any new database assignment.

In this chapter, we will create primary access tables. In the following sections, you'll look at the procedure of adding tables to an access database, including the extraordinarily complicated challenge of choosing the right records kind to assign to every discipline in a table. It's constantly an excellent idea to plan tables first, earlier than you operate the get entry to equipment to add tables to the database. Many tables, in particular small ones, actually don't require a lot of forethought before adding them to the database. In any case, now not an awful lot making plans is needed to layout a desk protecting research facts, inclusive of the names of towns and states. But, more complex entities, including clients and products, commonly require substantial idea and attempt to implement well.

Despite the fact that you can layout the desk without any forethought as you create it in get entry to, care- completely planning a database machine is a superb concept. You could make changes later, but doing so wastes time; commonly, the result is a machine that's tougher to preserve than one that you've planned nicely from the beginning. Within the following sections, we discover the brand new, blank table introduced to the chapter04.msaccdb database. It's crucial to apprehend the steps required to add new tables to an access database.

Designing a table

1. Create a new table
2. Enter field names, properties, data types and descriptions if you want
3. Select and set the primary key for the table
4. Create indexes for the field necessary
5. Now save the tables design

Usually talking, a few tables are in no way definitely completed. As users' needs trade or the commercial enterprise rules governing the application exchange, you would possibly find it vital to open an existing desk in design view. This book, like maximum books on MS Access, describes the manner of creating tables as if each table you ever work on is modern. The truth is, however, that most of the work that you do on an Access is completed on current gadgets in the database. Some of the ones objects you've brought yourself, at the same time as different gadgets may additionally have been brought by every other developer at a while in the beyond. However, the technique of preserving a current database aspect could be very tons the same as growing the equal object from scratch. Begin by means of choosing the Create tab at the Ribbon on the top of the Access display screen. The Create tab (proven in discern 4.1) carries all the equipment important to create not handiest tables, but also forms, reports, and other database objects.

Figure # 4.1

The Create tab contains tools necessary for adding new objects to your Access database.

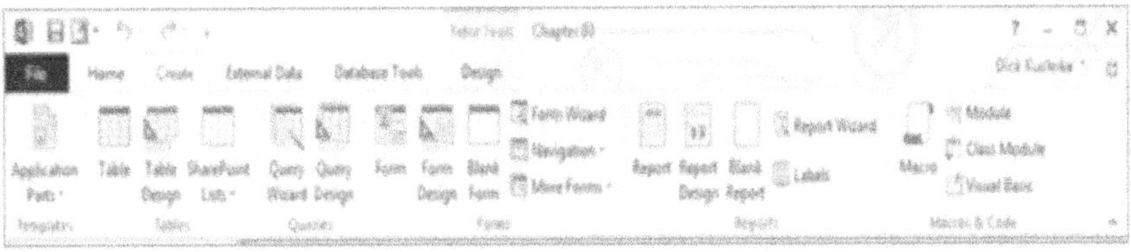

There are two main methods to add new tables to an get entry to database, each of which are invoked from the Tables group at the Create tab:

- Clicking the table button provides a table in Datasheet view to the database with one autonumber field named identity
- Clicking the table design button adds a table in design view to the database

For this case, we'll be the use of the table design button, but first, permit's take a look at the

Table button.

Clicking the table button provides a new table to the MS Access environment. The new table appears in Datasheet view inside the location to the right of the Navigation pane. The new table is proven in determine 4.2. Be aware that the new table seems in Datasheet view, with an identity column already inserted and a click to add column to the proper of the id field.

Figure # 4.2

The new table in Datasheet view.

The click to add column is supposed to allow clients to fast upload fields to a table. All you need to do is start entering facts within the new column. You assign the field a name by means of right clicking the field's heading, selecting Rename subject, and coming into a name for the field. In different words, constructing an get admission to table can be very much like growing a spreadsheet in Excel. After you've added the new column, the gear on the Fields tab of the Ribbon (shown in discern 4.3) allow you to set the precise facts kind for the sphere, alongside its formatting, validation regulations, and other houses.

Figure # 4.3

Field design tools are located on the Fields tab of the Ribbon.

The second one technique of adding new tables is to click on the desk design button inside the Tables group at the Create tab. Get entry to opens a new table in design view, permitting you to feature fields to the desk's layout. Figure 4.4 indicates a new table's layout after a few fields were introduced. Table layout view affords a quite greater deliberate technique to building access tables.

Figure # 4.4

A new table added in Design view.

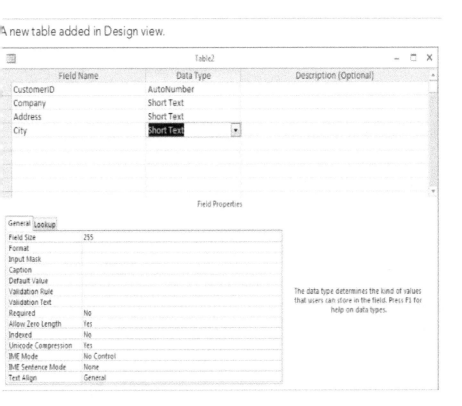

The table design is simple to apprehend, and every column is clearly labeled. On some distance left is the field name column, where you input the names of fields you add to the table. You assign a data type to every field in the table and (optionally) offer a description for the field. Statistics types are mentioned in detail later in this chapter.

For this exercising, you create the clients table for the Collectible Mini cars application. The fundamental layout of this table is printed in table 3.1. We cover the information of this table's design within the "creating tblclients" section, later in this chapter.

Table # 4.1: Mini Car Client's Table

Field name	Data type	Description
Clients ID	Auto number	Primary key
Agency	Short text	Employer contact
Address	Short text	Contact address
City	Short text	Contact city
State	Short text	Contact state
Zip code	Short text	Contact zip code
Phone	Short text	Contact phone
Fax	Short text	Contact fax
Email	Short text	Contact email
Website	Short text	Contact web address
Credit limit	Currency	Credit limit of customers in dollar
Current balance	Currency	Current balance of customers in dollars
Credit status	Short text	Description of customers credit status
Active	Y/N	Whether client is still buying or selling to mini cars

4.4 Design tab

Figure # 4.5

The Design tab of the Ribbon.

4.4.1 Primary key

Click on this button to designate which of the fields within the table you need to use because the tables primary key. Traditionally, the primary key seems on the top of the list of fields inside the table, but it may appear anywhere in the table's layout.

4.4.2 Insert row

Although it makes little difference to the database engine, many builders are fussy approximately the sequence of fields in a table. Many of the wizards in get entry to show the fields inside the identical order because the table. Keeping a address field over the city field can make developments much easier. Clicking the Insert Rows button inserts a blank row just above the position occupied by way of the mouse cursor. As an example, if the cursor is presently within the 2nd row of the table designer, clicking the Insert Rows button inserts an empty row within the 2nd role, shifting the present 2nd row to the 3rd position

4.4.3 Delete row

Clicking the Delete Rows button gets rid of a row from the table's design.

4.4.4 Property Sheet

Clicking the property Sheet button opens the property Sheet for the complete table (proven in figure 4.6). Those properties permit you to specify essential table traits, together with a validation rule to apply to the entire table, or an exchange sort order for the desk's information.

Figure # 4.6

The Property Sheet.

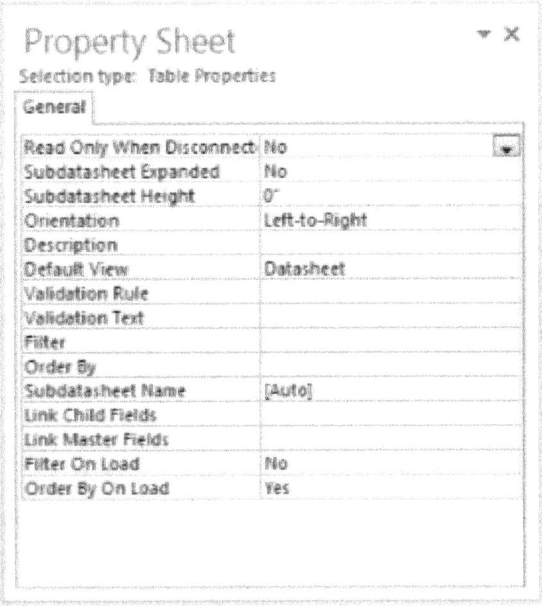

Property Sheet	▾ ✕
Selection type: Table Properties	
General	

Read Only When Disconnect	No
Subdatasheet Expanded	No
Subdatasheet Height	0"
Orientation	Left-to-Right
Description	
Default View	Datasheet
Validation Rule	
Validation Text	
Filter	
Order By	
Subdatasheet Name	[Auto]
Link Child Fields	
Link Master Fields	
Filter On Load	No
Order By On Load	Yes

4.4.5 Indexes

ndexes are discussed in a great deal more element within the "Indexing access ables" phase, later on this bankruptcy. Clicking the Indexes button opens the

Indexes conversation box, which permits you to specify the information of indexes at the fields in your table.

4.5 Working with fields

You create fields with the aid of coming into an area call and a subject information kind in the top area entry vicinity of the table layout window. The (optionally available) Description property may be used to signify the sphere's purpose. The outline appears within the popularity bar at the bottom of the display for the duration of records access and may be beneficial to humans working with the utility. After coming into every subject's call and records kind, you can in addition specify how every area is utilized by getting into properties within the field properties area.

4.6 Naming a discipline

An area call should be descriptive enough to become aware of the field to you because the developer, to the consumer of the system, and to MS Access. Field names ought to be long enough to quick identify the purpose of the field, however now not overly lengthy. (Later, as you enter validation guidelines or use the field name in a calculation, you'll need to save yourself from typing lengthy field names.)

To enter a subject name, role the pointer within the first row of the table design window beneath the sphere call column. Then type a valid field name, watching these guidelines:

- Field names may be from 1 to 64 characters in its length.
- Field name can include letters, numbers, and special characters, besides period (.),
  Exclamation mark (!), accent grave (`), and brackets ([]).

- Field names can consist of spaces. Spaces ought to be avoided in field names for some of
  The same motives you keep away from them in table names.
- You couldn't use low order ASCII character as an example Ctrl+J or Ctrl+L (ASCII values
  0 to 31).
- You mayn't begin with a blank space.

You can enter field names in uppercase, lowercase, or mixed case. In case you make a mistake even as typing the field name, function the cursor wherein you want to make a correction and kind the alternate. You can exchange a field name at any time, even if the table includes data.

Chapter 5

5.1 data types

When you enter a field, you must also decide what kind of records every of your fields will hold. In MS Access, you can pick any of several data types.

Short text

The short text data type holds facts that is virtually and simply characters (letters, numbers, punctuation). Names, addresses, and descriptions are all text data, as are numeric facts that aren't utilized in a calculation (inclusive of telephone numbers, Social safety numbers, and zip codes). Although you specify the scale of each quick textual content field within the property region, you could input no extra than 255 characters of information in any quick textual content area. Get right of entry to makes use of variable length fields to shop textual content records. If you designate a discipline to be 25 characters huge and you use simplest five characters for every report, then handiest enough room to save 5 characters is used on your database.

You'll find that the ACCDB database report would possibly fast grow quite huge, but textual content fields are commonly no longer the cause. However, it's correct practice to restriction quick textual content subject widths to the maximum you believe is likely for the sphere. Names can be complicated due to the fact pretty long names are not unusual in some cultures. But, it's a safe guess that a postal code can be fewer than 12 characters, while a U.S. state abbreviation is usually 2 characters. By limiting a short textual content field's width, you furthermore may limit the number of characters customers can input whilst the sphere is utilized in a form.

Long text

The long text data type holds a variable quantity of statistics up to 1GB. Long text data types use handiest as a lot memory as important for the data stored. So, if one record uses one hundred characters, some other requires only 10, and yet another wishes 3,000, you use only as plenty area as each report calls for. You don't specify a field length for the long text data type. Access allocates as a whole lot area as essential for the data.

Number

The wide variety of data type allows you to enter numeric information that is, numbers so one can be utilized in mathematical calculations or represent scalar portions consisting of stock counts. (when you have records with a view to be used in monetary calculations, use the currency information type, which plays calculations without rounding errors.)

The exact sort of numeric records stored in quite a number area is decided via the field size property. Design your tables very conservatively and permit for larger values than you ever assume to peer to your database. This isn't always to say that using the Double information type for all numeric fields is a good idea. The Double data type is very big (8 bytes) and is probably extremely slow when used in calculations or different numeric operations. Instead, the single data type might be best for most floating-point calculations, and long Integer is a great choice in which decimal points are irrelevant.

Large numbers

The large number data type holds values from -2^{63} to $2^{63}-1$. The ones are larger numbers than most of the people want. It turned into Access specially for compatibility with other databases which have this information type, in particular SQL Server.

In case you use massive range, be aware that not all variations of Access previous to 2019 support this data type. In case you're linking to or uploading from a database that makes use of this information type, take a look at support large range (Big Integer) facts type for connected/Imported Tables check container within the modern Database tab of access options.

Date/Time

The Date/Time statistics kind is a specialized range discipline for containing dates or times (or dates and instances). While dates are stored in a Date/Time subject, it's easy to calculate days between dates and different calendar operations. Date facts stored in Date/Time fields kind and filter properly as nicely. The Date/Time facts type holds dates from January 1, 100, to December 31, 9999.

Currency

The currency records kind is any other specialized number discipline. Currency numbers are not rounded throughout calculations and preserve 15 digits of precision to the left of the decimal factor and 4 digits to the proper. Because currency fields use a fixed decimal factor role, they're faster in numeric calculations than doubles.

Autonumber

The autonumber area is every other specialized variety data type. While an autonumber field is added to a table, access mechanically assigns a long integer

(32-bit) value to the field (starting at 1) and increments the value every time a document is introduced to the table. Instead (determined by way of the new Values property), the cost of the autonumber subject is a random integer that is automatically inserted into new records.

Only one autonumber field can appear in a table. As soon as assigned to a report, the cost of an autonumber discipline can't be changed programmatically or by means of the user. Autonumber fields are stored as a protracted Integer facts type and occupy 4 bytes. Autonumber fields can accommodate as much as 4,294,967,296 specific numbers extra than adequate because the primary key for maximum tables.

Yes/No

Yes/No fields receive simplest considered one of two viable values. Internally saved as −1 (yes) or 0 (No), the yes/No field is used to indicate on/off, yes/no, or true/false. A yes/No area occupies a single bit of storage.

5.2 OLE object

The OLE object field stores OLE information, exceedingly specialized binary items inclusive of word files, Excel spreadsheets, sound or video clips, and pics. The OLE item is created via a software that windows acknowledges as an OLE server and can be connected to the figure software or embedded in the get right of entry to desk. OLE items may be displayed best in bound object frames in get admission to bureaucracy and reviews. OLE fields can't be indexed.

Hyperlink

The hyperlink records type field holds combinations of text and numbers saved as text and used as a link cope with. It is able to have as much as four parts:

The textual content that looks in a control (typically formatted to look like a clickable hyperlink).

The cope with—the course to a document or web page.

Any sub-cope with within the record or page. An instance of a sub-cope with is a image on

A web page. Each a part of the link's address is separated with the aid of the pound sign (#).

The text that looks in the display tip while the consumer hovers over the hyperlink.

MS Access hyperlinks may even point to forms and reviews in different MS Access to databases. Which means that you may use a hyperlink to open a form or report in an external Access database and show the form or document at the person's computer.

Attachment

The Attachment statistics kind became introduced in get admission to 2007. In truth, the Attachment statistics type is one of the motives Microsoft modified the format of the MS Access to information record. The older MDB format is not able to accommodate attachments.

The Attachment data type is relatively complicated, compared to the alternative styles of Access fields, and it calls for a unique form of manipulate whilst displayed on Access field.

Calculated

A Calculated field holds an expression that may include numbers, text, fields from within the same table, and Access features. It cannot reference fields from different tables. "Calculated" isn't a data type despite the fact that access consists of it within the information kind listing. It has a Result Type property that determines what kind of facts the field holds. You would possibly use a Calculated field if you find you're appearing the same calculations in queries time and again. For instance, if you had a Taxable Amount field and a Sales Tax Rate field, you could create a Sales Tax Amount subject that multiplies them together.

The use of this field comes dangerously close to violating the third normal form. The field virtually shops the system and not the calculated price. However, this is what queries are for and you could locate that maintaining the information to your tables and the calculations in your queries is a good manner to organize your software application.

Lookup Wizard

The lookup Wizard data type inserts a subject that enables the end user to choose a value from every other table or from the results of a SQL statement. The values can also be supplied as a blend box or list box. At design time, the lookup Wizard leads the developer through the procedure of defining the research characteristics when this information is assigned to a field. As you drag an object from the lookup Wizard area list, a combo box or listing field is automatically created at the form. The listing box or mixture field also seems on a query datasheet that incorporates the field.

Chapter 6

6.1 Changing table design/layout

Even the high-quality planned table may additionally require changes now and again. You may find which you need to feature any other field, change a name of the field, exchange a field name or data type, or in reality rearrange the order of the fields names.

Although a table's layout can be modified at any time, special issues ought to accept to tables containing facts. Be careful of making adjustments that harm data in the table, which include making textual content fields smaller or converting the filed size belongings of range fields. You can constantly add new fields to a table without issues, but changing existing fields is probably a problem. And, with only a few exceptions, it's almost always an awful concept to change a field's name after a table has been positioned into use in an application.

Insertion of new field

To insert a new field, inside the tale design window, place your cursor on a current field, proper click on an area within the table design surface, and select Insert Rows, or just click the Insert Rows button on the layout tab of the Ribbon. A new row is added to the table, and current fields are driven pushed down. You could then input a new field definition. Inserting a field doesn't disturb different fields or present facts. When you have queries, forms, or reports that use the table, you may want to add the field to the ones objects as properly.

Deleting a field

There are three methods to delete a field. Even as the table is in design view:

- Pick the field by means of clicking the row selector and then press Delete.

- Right-click on the chosen field and choose Delete Rows from the shortcut menu.
- Select the field and click on the Delete Rows button from the equipment group on the
  Design tab of the Ribbon.

When you delete a field containing any data, you'll see a warning that you'll lose crucial data in the table for the selected in a field. If the table includes data, make sure which you want to eliminate the data for that field (column). You'll additionally should delete the identical field from queries, bureaucracy, reports, macros, and VBA code that use the field name.

In case you deleting a field, you must also fix all references to that area all through access. Due to the fact you could use a subject call in paperwork, queries, reports, and even table information validation, you should examine your gadget carefully to locate any instances in that you would possibly have used the precise field name.

Changing field location

The order of your fields, as entered inside the table layout view, determines the left to proper column collection inside the table's Datasheet view. If making a decision that your fields need to be rearranged, click on a subject selector and use the mouse to pull the sphere to its new area.

Converting a field name

You change a discipline's name by way of choosing the fields name within the table layout window and coming into a new name. Get right of entry to updates the table design routinely. As long as you're creating a new table, this process is straightforward. For current tables which can be referenced some other place in your software application, changing the field name can expose issues.

Changing field size

Creating a data size large is easy in a table layout. You definitely increase the field length belongings for text fields or specify an extraordinary subject size for number fields. You need to take note of the Decimal places belongings in wide variety fields to make certain you don't pick a new size that helps fewer decimal locations than you currently have.

Chapter 7

7.1 Selecting data with queries

7.1.1 Introducing queries

The word query comes from the Latin phrase quaerere, which means that "to ask or inquire." Over time, the word question has turn out to be synonymous with quiz, project, inquire, or question.

An MS Access query is a question that you ask approximately the information saved in Access tables. You buildup queries with the tools of MS access query. Your query may be a simple query about information in a single table, or it could be a greater complex query approximately information saved in numerous tables. As an example, you would possibly ask your database to expose you best vehicles that have been bought within the year of 2012. After you publish the query inside the shape of a question, Access returns most effective the data you have requested.

Creating query

When you create your tables and place records in them, you're able to work with queries. To begin a question, select the Create tab at the Ribbon, and click on the question layout button within the Queries organization. The underlying window is the question dressmaker. Floating on top of the query designer is the show table dialog box. The display table dialog field is modal, this means that which you ought to do something in the conversation container before continuing with the question. Earlier than you keep, you add the tables required for the question. In this example, tblproducts is highlighted and prepared to be added.

Figure # 7.1

The Show Table dialog box and the query design window.

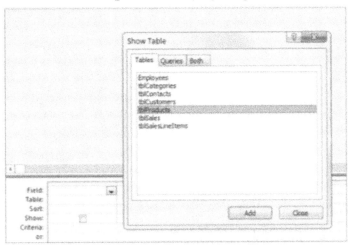

Getting rid of a table from the query is easy. Virtually right-click on the table within the question query designer and pick out dispose of table from the shortcut menu.

The query layout window has three primary views:

- Layout view: wherein you create the query
- Datasheet view: presentations the statistics again by the question
- SQL view: presentations the sq. Statement in the back of a question

The query designer consists of two sections:

- **The table/query pane:** this is in which tables or queries and their respective discipline lists are brought to the query's layout. You'll see a separate field listing for every item to add. Every field list includes the names of all the fields inside the respective table or query. You may resize a field listing by means of clicking the rims and dragging it to a special length. You can need to resize a field list so that each one of a table's fields are seen.

Figure # 7.2

The query design window with tblProducts added.

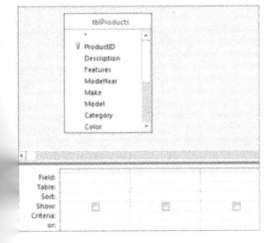

- **The query via layout (QBD) grid:** The QBD grid holds the field names Involved in the query and any criteria used to pick data. Each column within the
QBD grid incorporates facts about a single field from a table or query contained
Inside the top pane.

The QBD grid has six labeled rows:

- **Field:** this is in which field names are entered or delivered.
- **Table:** This row suggests the table the field in the table is from. That is beneficial in queries with multiple tables.
- **Sort:** This row enables sorting commands for the queries in the table or field.
- **Show:** This row determines whether to show the field inside the returned record set.
- **Criteria:** This row includes the criteria that clear out the lower back records.
- **Or:** This row is the first of a number of rows to which you could add a couple of query standards.

The query tools design Ribbon incorporates many buttons precise to building and working with queries. Even though each button is explained.

Figure # 7.3

The Query Tools Design Ribbon.

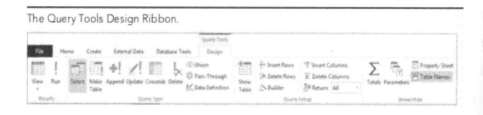

- **View:** Switches among the Datasheet view and design view within the question layout window. The View drop down control additionally enables you to show the underlying SQL statement in the back of the query.
- **Run:** Runs the query. Shows a select question's datasheet, serving the same function as choosing Datasheet View from the View button. However, whilst running with action queries, the Run button performs

the operations (append, make table, and so on) detailed with the aid of the question.

- **Select:** Clicking the select button transforms the opened question into a choose query.

- **Make table, Append, replace, Crosstab, and Delete:** each of those buttons specifies the type of question you're building. In most instances, you transform a pick question into a movement question by way of clicking one of these buttons.
- **Display table:** Opens the display desk dialog container.

Chapter 8

8.1 Joins

You'll often want to build queries that require or greater related tables to be joined to achieve the desired results. As an instance, you could need to enroll in a worker table to a transaction table in order create a record that incorporates both transaction details and information at the personnel who logged into those transactions. The sort of join used will decide the information a good way to be output.

Getting to know joins

There are three basic varieties of joins: inner joins, left outer joins, and right outer joins.

Inner joins: An internal join operation tells Access to pick handiest those data from each tables that have matching values in both tables. Facts with values inside the joined field that don't seem in both tables are neglected from the query effects.

An inner join operation will choose simplest the data which have matching values in each tables. The arrows point to the information that will be included within the consequences.

Figure # 8.1

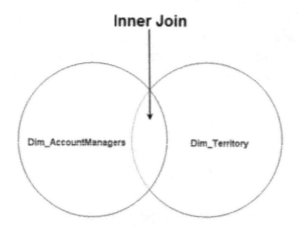

Left outer joins: A left outer join operation (on occasion known as a "left be a part of") tells get entry to pick all the data from the primary table regardless of if the data matches or not in the second table that have matching values within the joined operation virtually.

A left outer be part of operation will pick out all information from the primary table and simplest those data from the second table that have matching values in each tables. The arrows factor to the facts with the intention to be blanketed in the effects.

Figure # 8.2

Left Join

Dim_AccountManagers

Dim_Territory

Right outer joins: A right outer join (once in a while known as a "right join" just) tells get Access to choose all the data from the second one table no matter matching and most effective the ones records from the primary table that have matching values inside the joined subject.

A right outer join Access all the information from the second one table and handiest those data from the first table that have matching values in both tables. The arrows point to the records to be able to be included within the results.

Figure # 8.3

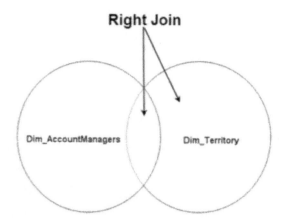

By means of default, an Access query returns most effective information where information exists on both aspects of a relationship (inner join). As an instance, a query that extracts data from the Contacts table and the income table only returns facts where contacts have sincerely located income and will no longer display contacts who haven't yet placed a sale. If a contact record isn't matched with the aid of at least one income file, the touch facts isn't back by means of the query. Which means that, occasionally, the query won't return all of the records you assume. Despite the fact that that is the maximum commonplace be part of kind among tables in a query, users every so often want to peer all of the data in a table regardless of whether those data are matched in another table. In reality, users frequently need to mainly see records that aren't matched on the alternative side of the join. Do not forget a sales branch that desires to recognize all the contacts that have no longer made a sale inside the last year. You should regulate the default question join characteristics on the way to process this form of query.

You can create joins between tables in those three approaches:

- By using growing relationships between the tables whilst you design the database.
- By using deciding on two tables for the query which have a subject in common that has the same call and information type in both tables. The field is a primary key field in one in all the tables.
- By way of enhancing the default be a part of behavior.

The first two methods occur robotically inside the query design window. Relationships among tables are displayed in the query designer while you add the related tables to a query. It additionally creates an automatic join between tables that have a not unusual area, so long as that field is a primary key in one of the tables and the allow Autojoin preference is chosen (by using default) inside the alternatives conversation field.

If relationships are set inside the Relationships window, you may not see the autojoin if:

- The two tables have a common subject; however, it isn't the same call.
- A desk isn't associated and mayn't be logically associated with the opposite table (for example, tblcustomers can't at once be part of the tblsaleslineitems table).

When you have two tables that aren't associated and also you need to enroll in them in a query, use the query layout window. Becoming a member of tables within the query layout window does no longer create a permanent relationship among the tables; as an alternative, join relationship applies most effective to the tables even as the query operates.

Chapter 9

9.1 Operators and Expressions

9.1.1 Introducing the operators

Operators permit you to evaluate values, positioned textual content strings together, layout data, and carry out an extensive variety of duties. You use operators to train access to perform a specific action against one or extra operands. The combination of operators and operands is known as an expression. You'll use operators each time you create an equation in get entry to. For instance, operators specify statistics validation rules in desk homes, create calculated fields in bureaucracy and reviews, and specify standards in queries.

9.2 types of operators

Operators can be grouped into the subsequent types:

- Comparison
- Boolean (logical)
- Miscellaneous
- String
- Mathematical

9.2.1 Mathematical operators

Mathematical operators are also known as mathematics operators, due to the fact they're used for appearing numeric calculations. By definition, you use mathematical operators to paintings with numbers as operands. When you work with mathematical operators, numbers can be any numeric facts kind. The range may be a steady fee, the value of a variable, or a field's contents. You operate these numbers individually or combine them to create complex expressions.

There are seven primary mathematical operators:

+ Addition

− Subtraction

* Multiplication

/ department

\ Integer department ^ Exponentiation Mod Modulo

Addition Operator

For calculated fields in a query.

[tax amount] + [price]

Subtraction Operator

[Amount] + [Amount] * [Discount percentage]

Multiplication Operator

To calculate the total price of several items having same price.

[price] * [Quantity of product]

Division Operator

To determine the individual persons payoff.

21 / 3

Exponentiation Operator

Raise number to the power of the exponent.

$4 \times 4 \times 4$ that is 4^3

9.2.2 Comparison operators

Contrast operators evaluate two values or expressions in an equation. There are six fundamental assessment operators:

= equal

<> not equal

< less than

<= less than or identical to

> greater than

>= greater than or equal to

Equal operator

This operator returns true if both of the expressions are same.

[category] = "Audi" returns true if category is Audi otherwise will return false.

Not equal operator

[category] < > "Audi" returns true if the category is anything but Audi.

.2.3 String operators

here are three types of string operators.

- Concatenates operand &
- Operands are similar LIKE
- Operands are dissimilar NOT LIKE

9.2.4 Boolean operators

Boolean operators (additionally referred to as logical operators) are used to create multiple conditions in expressions. Like comparison operators, these operators constantly return false, true, or Null. Boolean operators consist of the subsequent:

- And returns true whilst both Expression1 and Expression2 are true.
- Or returns true when either Expression1 or Expression2 is true.
- Not returns true while the Expression isn't true.
- Xor returns true whilst both Expression1 or Expression2 is authentic, however now not both.
- Eqv returns true whilst both Expression1 and Expression2 are authentic or each are
  False.
- Imp performs bitwise comparisons of identically placed bits in two numerical
  Expressions.

Chapter 10

10.1 Aggregate Queries

An aggregate query, sometimes referred to as a collection by means of query, is a sort of query you may construct to help you quick congregate into group and summarize your data. With a select query, you may retrieve records most effective as they seem to your facts source. But with an aggregate query, you may retrieve a summary snapshot of your facts that indicates you totals, averages, counts, and greater.

Create aggregate query

To get a company understanding of what an aggregate query does, don't forget the following scenario: You've simply been requested to offer the sum of general sales with the aid of length. In response to this request, begin a question in layout view and bring in the Dim Dates period and Dim Transactions. Line Total fields, as proven in figure 10.1. If you run this query as is, you'll get every record to your information set in preference to the precis you want.

Figure # 10.1

Running this query will return all the records in your data set, not the summary you need.

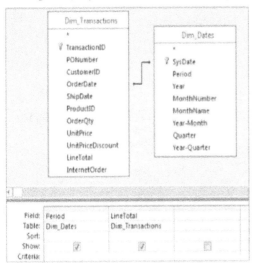

So, one can get a price of sales by means of duration, you'll need to set off Totals to your layout grid. To do that, go to the Ribbon and pick the layout tab, and then click on the Totals button. As you can see in figure 10.2, when you've activated Totals on your layout grid, you'll see a new row on your grid called total. The overall row tells access which aggregate feature to apply when appearing aggregation on the desired fields.

Word that the entire row consists of the phrases group by using under every field on your grid. Because of this all comparable records in a field might be grouped to provide you with a unique records object. The concept right here is to modify the combination capabilities inside the total row to correspond with the analysis you're trying to perform. In this state of affairs, you want to organization all of the intervals to your records set and then sum the revenue in each period. Consequently, you'll need to use the group by aggregate feature for the duration discipline, and the Sum aggregate feature for the Line Total field. Because the default selection for Totals is the group by using feature, no alternate is needed for the length discipline. But, you'll need to alternate the aggregate characteristic for the Line Total subject from institution by means of Sum. This tells Access which you need to sum the sales figures within the Line Total field, not group them. To trade the aggregate feature, truly click the entire drop-down listing beneath the Line Total subject, shown in figure 10.3, and pick out Sum. At this factor, you could run your query.

Figure # 10.2

Activating Totals in your design grid adds a Total row to your query grid that defaults to Group By.

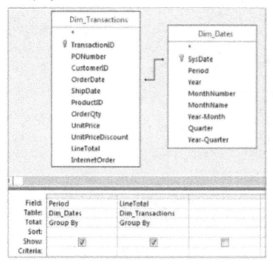

Figure # 10.3

Change the aggregate function under the LineTotal field to Sum.

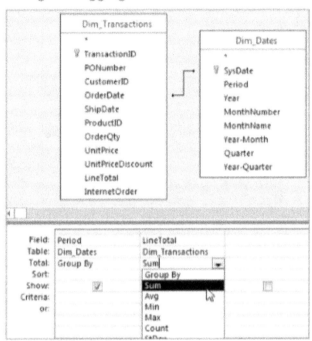

Figure # 10.4

Period	SumOfLineTotal
201107	$1,282,530.35
201108	$3,008,547.90
201109	$2,333,985.05
201110	$1,982,360.35
201111	$4,338,025.75
201112	$3,457,253.40
201201	$1,928,725.30
201202	$3,712,032.10
201203	$3,109,211.70
201204	$2,224,498.50
201205	$4,308,899.75

9.2 Group By

The group by aggregate function all the records in the specified area into particular organizations. Here are some things to hold in thoughts while the usage of the group by through the aggregate functions:

- **Access performs the** Group by using function in your mixture query earlier than every other aggregation. In case you're acting a group with the aid of at the side of some other aggregate characteristic, the Group by the aid of function will be proffered first. MS Access it just groups the period field first then summing the line total field

- **MS Access sorts every group by the fields in ascending order.** Until otherwise distinct, any area tagged as a set via field tagged as group by in ascending order. In case your query has a couple of group by using fields, each subject can be sorted in ascending order starting with the leftmost discipline.

- **Access treats a couple of group by fields as one unique item.** This question counts all of the transactions that have been logged within the 201201 length.

9.3 Sum, Avg, rely, stdev, Var

Those combination capabilities all perform mathematical calculations against the records in your chosen discipline. It's essential to notice that those capabilities exclude any statistics that are set to null. In different words, these mixture functions forget about any empty cells.

Sum: Calculates the full value of all the records inside the certain subject or grouping. This characteristic will work best with the subsequent information types: autonumber, currency, Date/Time, and number.

Avg: Calculates the average of all of the data inside the targeted designated or grouping. This feature will paintings most effective with the following information kinds: autonumber, currency, Date/Time, and wide variety.

Count: Counts the quantity of entries within the distinct field or grouping. This feature works with all data types.

Stdev: Calculates the same old deviation throughout all records inside the distinctive discipline or grouping. This characteristic will paintings best with the following records kinds: autonumber, Currency, Date/Time, and number.

Var: Calculates the amount via which all the values within the detailed field or grouping vary from the average cost of the group. This feature will work handiest with the subsequent data types: autonumber, currency, Date/Time, and variety.

9.4 Min, Max, First, last

Unlike different mixture capabilities, these features examine all of the facts in the special area or grouping and go back a single cost from the group.

Min: Returns the price of the file with the bottom cost inside the distinctive field or grouping. This function will work only with the following facts types: autonumber, currency, Date/Time, number, and textual content.

Max: Returns the price of the file with the maximum value in the record or column grouping. This characteristic will work most effective with the subsequent facts types: autonumber, forex, Date/Time, range, and textual content.

First: Returns the price of the first record inside the specific column or grouping. This function works with all kinds of data types.

Last: Returns the value of the remaining file in the precise field or grouping. This function works with all data types.

9.5 Expression where

One of the steadfast guidelines of aggregate queries is that each area ought to have an aggregation carried out in opposition to it. But, in some conditions you'll must use a subject as a utility that is, use a field to simply carry out a calculation or apply a clear out. Those fields are a means to get to the final evaluation you're looking for, as opposed to part of the final analysis. In those situations, you'll use the Expression characteristic or the where clause. The Expression feature and the in which clause are precise in that they don't carry out any grouping action per se.

Expression: The Expression combination feature is normally carried out whilst you are making use of custom calculations or other features in a mixture question. Expression tells access to carry out the specified custom calculation on every character record or organization one.

Where: The where clause lets in you to apply a criterion to a discipline that is not blanketed for your combination question, efficaciously making use of a clear out in your analysis.

Note which you're using aliases on this question: "revenue" for the Line Total subject and "fee" for the custom calculation defined here. The usage of an alias of "revenue" gives the sum of Line Total a user pleasant name.

Chapter 11

11.1 MS Access Macros

Macros have been part of access on account that the start. As get right of entry to developed as a development tool, the visual primary for applications (VBA) programming language have become the same old in automating MS Access database applications. Macros in versions previous to access 2007 lacked variables and mistakes handling, which precipitated many developers to desert macros altogether. Get entry to nowadays has those, which make macros a much more possible alternative to VBA than in preceding versions. If you're developing a database to be used on the web, or if you aren't a VBA guru however you continue to want to personalize the movements that your utility executes, then constructing based macros is the solution.

Introduction to Macros

A macro is a tool that allows you to automate responsibilities in Access database. It's distinctive from word's Macro Recorder, which helps you to record a chain of actions and play them returned later. (It's additionally distinctive from phrase in that phrase macros are sincerely VBA code, whereas access macros are something very special.) Access macros allow you to carry out defined moves and upload capability on your forms and reviews. Think of macros as a simplified, step cleared programming language. You build a macro as a list of movements to carry out, and you make a decision while you need those movements to arise. Constructing macros consists of choosing actions from a drop-down listing and then filling in the motion's arguments (values that offer facts to the movement). Macros allow you to pick actions without writing a single line of VBA code. The macro actions are a subset of commands VBA presents. The majority find it less difficult to construct a macro than to write VBA code. In case you're no longer acquainted with VBA, constructing macros is a notable stepping stone to studying some of the instructions available to you at the same time as providing brought fee to your get admission to programs. Suppose you need to construct a primary shape with buttons that open the alternative forms for your utility. You can add a button to the form, construct a macro that opens some other form in your software, after which assign this macro to the button's click occasion. The macro may be a standalone item that looks inside the Navigation pane, or it is able to be an embedded item that is part of the event itself.

Creating Macro

An easy manner to demonstrate a way to create macros is to build one which shows a message box that says, "hello world" To create a new stand by standalone macro, click the Macro button at the Macros & Code organization on the Create tab of the Ribbon.

Figure # 11.1

Use the Macro button on the Create tab to build a new stand-alone macro.

Clicking the Macro button opens the macro builder. To start with, the macro builder is nearly featureless. The best component in the Macro Builder is a drop-down list of macro moves.

To the proper of the Macro Builder you could see the movement Catalog. There are dozens of different macro moves and knowing which motion to apply for a selected mission can be an issue. The action Catalog provides a tree view of all to be had macro movements and allows you understand which action is wanted to perform a selected task. Select Message Box from the drop-down listing in the macro builder. The macro builder changes to show a place wherein you enter the arguments (Message, Beep, type, and name) related to the Message Box motion.

Set the arguments as follows:

- **Message:** hello world!
- **Beep:** No
- **Type:** None
- **Name:** A simple Macro

Figure # 11.2

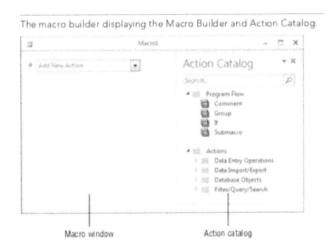

The macro builder displaying the Macro Builder and Action Catalog.

The Message argument defines the textual content that appears in the message box and is the best argument that is required and has no default. The Beep argument determines whether or not a beep is heard whilst the message container appears. The sort argument sets which icon appears inside the message box: None, essential, caution?, warning!, or facts. The title argument defines the textual content that looks in the message container's title bar.

Figure # 11.3

The Hello World! macro uses the MessageBox action to display a message.

To run the macro, click the Run button within the tools institution of the layout tab of the Ribbon. (The Run button seems like a large purple exclamation factor on a ways left of the Ribbon.) When you create a new macro or trade an existing macro, you'll be triggered to save the macro. In reality, you have to save the macro before access runs it for you. When caused, click sure to store it, provide a name (such as "macros helloworld"), and click on adequate. The macro runs and dis- plays a message field with the arguments you special.

Figure # 11.4

Running the Hello World! macro displays a message box.

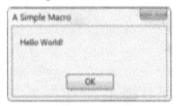

You could also run the macro from the Navigation pane. Close the macro builder and display the Macros group in the Navigation pane. Double-click the macros helloworld macro to run it. You'll see the identical message field that displayed when you ran the macro from the design window. Note that the message container constantly seems close to the middle of the display screen and blocks you from working with Access until you click good enough. Those are integrated behaviors of the message container item and are same in each regard to a message field displayed from VBA code. Whilst you're satisfied with the hello world! Macro, click the near button within the top-right corner of the macro builder to go back to the Access window.

Chapter 12

12.1 Access VBA

Most Access developers macros now after which. Despite the fact that macros offer a brief and clean manner to automate an application, writing visible basic for packages (VBA) modules is the excellent way to create packages. VBA offers data Access, looping and branching, and different features that macros virtually don't assist or as a minimum not with the power most builders want. On this forms, you learn how to use VBA to extend the energy and value of your applications.

12.2 Introducing visual simple

Visual basic for packages (VBA) is the programming language built into Microsoft Access. VBA is shared amongst all the workplace office applications, which includes Excel, word, Outlook, PowerPoint, and even Visio. In case you aren't already a VBA programmer, getting to know the VBA syntax and a way to hook VBA into the Access occasion version is a definite career builder. VBA is a key element in maximum professional Access applications. Microsoft presents VBA in access due to the fact VBA provides huge flexibility and power to Access database applications. Without a full composed programming language like VBA, access packages might ought to rely upon the truly restricted set of actions supplied by means of Access macros. Despite the fact that macro programming also provides flexibility to access applications, VBA is a good deal easier to paintings with whilst you're programming complex records management functions or sophisticated person interface necessities. In case you're new to programming, attempt not to come to be frustrated or crushed by way of the seeming complexity of the VBA language. As with all new skill, you are much higher off approaching VBA programming by using taking it one step at a time. You need to study exactly what VBA can do for you and your packages, at the side of the overall syntax, announcement shape, and the way to compose procedures using the VBA language.

Chapter 13

13.1 Integration of Microsoft Access with SharePoint

SharePoint is Microsoft's collaborative server environment, providing equipment for sharing files and statistics throughout numerous groups inside your company network. SharePoint is typically deployed on an organization's network as a series of SharePoint web sites. A SharePoint website is configured as an intranet site, giving diverse departments the ability to govern their personal safety, workgroups, documents, and facts. Those web sites can be nested within different websites in a hierarchical style. As with any other website, the pages inside a SharePoint site are available via a URL that the person can get entry to via a well-known web browser. Although SharePoint is maximum regularly used for sharing files, records tables, and other content control responsibilities, SharePoint is often carried out many other applications as an instance, to address the documentation required for product improvement. A SharePoint web site committed to improvement mission easily handles the challenge initiation, monitoring, and development reporting tasks. Due to the fact SharePoint without problems handles sincerely any type of document, mission drawings, motion pictures, schematics, snap shots, and so on, may be delivered to the task's SharePoint web site for overview and remark by means of venture contributors.

Companies regularly use SharePoint for dispensing human aid and coverage documents. Because SharePoint offers user and institution degree safety, it's pretty clean to supply a particular branch access to a SharePoint page at the same time as denying different users access to the same web page. SharePoint also logs changes to files and supports a take a look check in/check out paradigm for controlling who is eligible to make modifications to current documents and who's allowed to post new files and files.

Conclusion

MS access has a lot of advantages over other database and it provides you with certain benefits if you have designed the data base really well **Prevention of Human error** MS Access catches inconsistencies caused by human blunders. As an example, your group may additionally have entered the equal patron below distinctive names via accident. (suppose "Grand Rapids Heating & Plumbing" vs. "Grand Rapids Heating"). Whilst this takes place, it is tough to drag all of the information you need for a purchaser. Microsoft Access to prevents those kinds of human errors. **Create person Interfaces** The "consumer interface" is the display screen your personnel will see after they input or edit records. In Access, you are able to create paperwork that simplest show the fields important for employees to do their jobs. This also gives your company better facts security. That way, your employees don't have complete get right of entry to on your corporation records. **Proportion Your Findings** certain sorts of records can tell your enterprise decisions transferring ahead. For instance, you may need to look what number of new leads you've got gotten after an advertising marketing campaign. One of the most important benefits of Microsoft Access to is that it is simple to proportion your findings with others. While you make a document in Microsoft access, you may print, export, or email it to other participants of your crew. That way, you'll be capable of share your findings and collaborate quite simply.

CPSIA information can be obtained
at www.ICGtesting.com
Printed in the USA
BVHW082101030521
606340BV00006B/1495

9 781802 262780